I REMEMBER

BORIS PASTERNAK

I REMEMBER

Sketch for an Autobiography

———

TRANSLATED WITH A PREFACE AND NOTES

BY David Magarshack

WITH AN ESSAY ON

❯ TRANSLATING SHAKESPEARE ❰

TRANSLATED BY

Manya Harari

HARVARD UNIVERSITY PRESS

CAMBRIDGE, MASSACHUSETTS

LONDON, ENGLAND

1983

This Harvard University Press paperback
is published by arrangement with Pantheon
Books, Inc.

Library of Congress Cataloging in Publication Data

Pasternak, Boris Leonidovich, 1890–1960.
  I remember.

  Translation of: Avtobiograficheskiĭ ocherk.
  1. Pasternak, Boris Leonidovich, 1890–1960—Biography.
  2. Poets, Russian—20th century—Biography. I. Title.
PG3476.P27Z46313   1983   891.71'42   83–10764
ISBN 0–674–43950–3 (pbk.)

CONTENTS

5

ILLUSTRATIONS

*Illustrations reproduced by courtesy of The Pushkin Club, London,
and Giangiacomo Feltrinelli Editore, Milan.*

PREFACE

Boris Pasternak's autobiographical sketch is the most outspoken and heart-searching document a great poet has ever written. It takes courage to dismiss, as Pasternak does, most of his literary output of the twenty-odd years that followed the publication in 1914 of his first volume of verse, *A Twin in the Clouds,* with the dry remark, "I do not like my style up to 1940"; but it takes even greater courage, knowing the sort of aura of sanctity that hangs over the name of Mayakovsky in the Soviet Union, to declare that he rejects half of Mayakovsky, or, even more bluntly, that Mayakovsky was being "propagated" by the Communist Government "like potatoes in the reign of Catherine the Great."

Like *Safe Conduct,* his first attempt at autobiography, published in 1931 and now rejected by him as "spoilt by unnecessary mannerisms," Pasternak's autobiography does not pretend to cover every important aspect of his life; it tells very little of his personal life and treads very warily over the political persecutions of which he, too, has been, and, of course, still is, the victim. What it does give is a glimpse into the formative years of his childhood and adolescence and a few seemingly disconnected, but from the point of view of his artistic development and growth deeply significant, scenes from his life, including a fleeting vision of Tolstoy's body at the wayside station of Astapovo and of his wife, the foolish and misguided countess, trying to justify her husband's flight from her.

It is perhaps not surprising that Boris Pasternak, whose father, Leonid Pasternak, was an eminent painter and whose mother, Rosa Kaufman Pasternak, was a highly talented concert pianist, should have decided to devote his life to the pursuit of the arts. What is surprising is that, having fallen under the influence of Scriabin and tried his hand at composition, he should have given up music entirely and, after a rather abortive attempt at the study of philosophy at Moscow and Marburg Universities, dedicated himself wholly to poetry. His own account of this dramatic break with music, interesting as it is, does not completely explain this purposeful abandonment of one art in favor of another. No doubt the poet had always lain dormant in him, but it must have been the revolt against "the old forms" in art, the desire, as he puts it, "to challenge the accepted conventions of poetic expression," which took such a violent form among the young Russian poets at the beginning of the present century, that exercised a powerful attraction on a poet like Pasternak. He was only too eager to join in the fray between the numerous camps of *avant-garde* poets who proclaimed their messianic missions under all sorts of exotic names. It is hard to find any reasonable explanation of the fury in their denunciations of one another that animated the different groups of futurists, symbolists, acmeists, and many other adherents of art

isms of those days. The only tangible evidence of this
clash of isms has been left by a man of genius who
took no part in it. In *The Seagull,* written toward the
end of the nineteenth century, Anton Chekhov re-
created in Konstantin Treplyov the angry young man
who revolts against the "old forms" of literary expression, the type of literary rebel of those days. In his play
Chekhov also furnished a plausible explanation of the
fierceness with which most of them attacked their
enemies, who, in turn, branded them as "decadents":
it was the haunting realization of their own mediocrity
that redoubled the fury of their denunciations, *that*
and the general feeling of impending catastrophe that
was to overtake a tottering political and social order
which obsessed the minds of the Russian intelligentsia
long before the actual collapse and disintegration of
the Tsarist regime. It was a time when all sorts of
weird, mystical beliefs flourished among the Russian
thinkers and writers, including that of the coming of
Antichrist and the imminent end of the world. Solovyov, the mystic and poet, who had apocalyptic dreams
of the end of the world and who had a vision of Sophia,
Divine Wisdom, in the Reading Room of the British
Museum, gave voice to this feeling by declaring that
"the end is already near, the unexpected will soon be
accomplished." Blok, the greatest poet of that epoch,
who actually believed that Solovyov's Sophia or Divine
Wisdom had been reincarnated in his fiancée, com-
menting on the Messina earthquake of 1908, wrote that

"if the ancient Scylla and Charybdis vanished from the earth, there is in the heart of the earth a more terrible Scylla and Charybdis lurking for all of us and all we can do is to put on mourning and celebrate our sorrow in the fact of the catastrophe. . . ." Another characteristic of the thinkers and poets of those days was that they were all "looking for a sign." "In real life," as Pasternak puts it, "I thought everything must be a miracle, everything must be predestined from above. . . ."

It was in this tense and highly charged atmosphere, where every kind of "mystery and deception" proliferated, that Pasternak began his literary career. From the rather vague reference in *Safe Conduct* it would appear that it was at the end of May, 1914, that his meeting with Mayakovsky took place in a coffeeshop on the Arbat. At that time both belonged to "two hostile futuristic groups." The ferment of ideas of those days left its imprint on Pasternak's poetry, as indeed it did on Russian poetry as a whole, including that of Alexander Blok, and his dislike of the style of his books up to 1940 is no doubt to be attributed to the complete break with his past after 1940. These earlier works include: *A Twin in the Clouds,* 1914–16; *Above the Barriers,* 1917; *My Sister, Life,* 1922 (first published in Berlin); *Themes and Variations,* 1923; *The Year 1905* and *Lieutenant Schmidt,* 1927; *Safe Conduct,* 1931; *Spektorsky* and *Second Birth,* 1932; four prose stories published in one volume in 1925 (*The Childhood of Luverse,* 1918, *Il Tratto di Apelle,* 1915; *Let-*

ters from Tula, 1918, and *Aerial Ways,* 1924) and reprinted under the title *Aerial Ways* in 1931. After 1940, Pasternak published: *In Early Trains,* 1942, *The Death of a Sapper,* 1943, and after a long interval during which he was mainly working at translations, his great novel *Doctor Zhivago,* "a piece of my life," as he told a French writer, with its supplement of poems, published abroad in translation, 1957–58.

There can be little doubt and, indeed, Pasternak makes it abundantly clear in *Doctor Zhivago,* that he had turned to translation chiefly as a consequence of the hostility to his creative work of the Soviet ruling circles and their mouthpieces in the press. Apart from his early translation of Kleist's comedy, *The Broken Jug,* which he himself condemns so unequivocally, and some Rilke poems which he mentions here, Pasternak's translations cover a vast field of poetry, including works by Goethe (*Faust*), Verhaeren, Verlaine, Shelley, some Georgian poets, and, of course, Shakespeare. Two volumes of his translations of Shakespeare's plays were published in Moscow in 1949. They include: *Othello, King Lear, Antony and Cleopatra, Hamlet, Romeo and Juliet,* and the two parts of *Henry IV.* He has since translated other plays, including *Macbeth.*

It is, however, his poetry written during recent years that shows his complete emancipation from the influences of the tumultuous years before and after the October Revolution. In them he achieves a compactness and lucidity of style that surpasses anything that he had written before. One day these poems of Pasternak's will certainly be put beside the finest productions of the Russian poetic genius. At present they have not even been published.

D. M.

INFANCY

1

In *Safe Conduct,* an autobiographical essay written in the twenties, I have analyzed the circumstances that made me what I am. Unfortunately, the book is spoilt by unnecessary mannerisms, the common fault of those years.

In the present sketch I shall not be able to avoid retelling certain things, though I shall do my best not to repeat myself.

2

I was born in Moscow on January 29, 1890 (O.S.), in Lyzhin's house, opposite the Theological Seminary in Oruzheyny [Arsenal] Lane. I find it difficult to explain, but I can still remember something of my walks in the autumn with my wet nurse in the seminary park. The soaking wet paths under heaps of fallen leaves, the ponds, the artificial hillocks, and the painted iron railings of the seminary, the games and fights of laughing, boisterous seminarists during the longer breaks.

Straight across the gates of the seminary stood a two-storied brick house with a yard for cabbies and our apartment over the gateway above the arc of its vaulted ceiling.

3

My sensations of infancy are made up of the elements of panic and ecstasy. Their colorful fairyland atmosphere stems from two central images which united everything and dominated everything: the image of the stuffed bears in the carriage establishments in Coachmaker's Yard, and the image of P. P. Konchalovsky, the broad-shouldered, hirsute, low-voiced, good-natured giant of a publisher, his family, and the pencil, pen, and India ink drawings of Serov, Vrubel, the Vasnetsov father and brothers, which hung in the rooms of his apartment.

The district itself was rather disreputable. It included such slums as Tverskie and Yamskie Streets, the Truba, and the Tsvetnoy lanes. Again and again I found myself dragged away by the hand. Some things were not good for me to know, others were not good for me to hear. But my nurses and nannies could not bear solitude, and then we found ourselves surrounded by a motley company. At midday, too, the mounted police were drilled on the square of the Znamensky barracks.

From this intercourse with beggars and women pilgrims, from this neighboring world of the world's spurned and rejected and the things that happened to them and their hysterical wailings on the near-by boulevards, I acquired much too early—and retained for the rest of my life—a feeling of terrifying and breath-taking pity for woman and an even more unendurable pity for my parents, who would die before me and whom I would have to save from the tortures of hell by doing something unimaginably wonderful, something that had never, never been done before.

4

When I was three, we moved to a government apartment in the School of Painting, Sculpture, and Architecture in Myasnitsky Street, opposite the General Post Office. The apartment was in a wing of the house, inside the yard and standing apart from the main building.

The main building, which was old and beautiful, was remarkable in many ways. It had been spared by the fire of Moscow in 1812. A century earlier, in the reign of Catherine the Great, the house was the secret meeting place of a Masonic lodge. The house was at the corner of Myasnitsky Street and Yushkov Lane, and its curved façade had a semicircular balcony with columns. The spacious balcony formed a nichelike recess in the wall, communicating by a door with the assembly hall. From it one could look down the whole length of Myasnitsky Street, disappearing in the distance in the direction of the railway stations.

From this balcony the people who lived in the house watched in 1894 the funeral procession of Alexander

III, and afterwards, two years later, separate scenes of the coronation celebrations at the beginning of the reign of Nicholas II.

Students and teachers were there. My mother held me by the hand in the crowd at the balcony railings. At her feet was a sheer drop into an abyss. At the bottom of the abyss, the empty street, strewn with sand, was in a state of suspended animation. The military bustled about rapping out orders, which, however, did not reach the ears of the spectators on the balcony, as though the dead silence of the thousands of people holding their breath, pushed back to the very edge of the pavements by the drawn-up lines of soldiers, absorbed every sound as completely as water is absorbed by sand. Church bells began ringing slowly and dolefully. A sea of hands rose like a wave in the distance which rolled on and on, farther and farther. Moscow was taking off her hat and crossing herself. To the accompaniment of the funereal ringing of church bells, which seemed to come from every direction, the head of an endless procession hove into sight: troops, clergy, black-caparisoned, plumed horses, a catafalque of fabulous splendor, heralds in strange costumes of another age. And the procession marched on and on and the façades of the buildings were covered in strip after strip of crepe and dressed all over in black cloth, and the mourning flags flew droopingly at half-mast.

The spirit of pageantry was inseparable from the

school, which was under the authority of the Ministry of the Imperial Court. The Grand Duke Sergey Alexandrovich was its patron, and he was present at its speech-days and exhibitions. The Grand Duke was lean and lanky. Covering their sketchbooks with their hats, my father and Serov used to draw caricatures of him at the receptions given by the Golitzins and the Yakunchikovs, whenever he was present.

5

A small house stood in the yard, opposite the gate, leading into a small garden with very old trees among the outbuildings, sheds, and stables. Downstairs, in the basement, hot luncheons were served for the students. The staircase was always full of the fumes of fat in which the pasties and cutlets were fried. The door of our apartment was on the next landing. The registrar of the art school lived on the story above.

This is what I read fifty years later, quite recently, many years after the Soviet regime had come into being, in N. S. Rodionov's book, *Moscow in the Life and Work of L. N. Tolstoy,* on page 125, in a reference to the year 1894:

"On November 23rd, Tolstoy and his daughters paid a visit to the painter L. O. Pasternak at the School of Painting, Sculpture, and Architecture, where Pasternak was the Principal. They went to a concert in which Pasternak's wife and the Professors of the Conservatory, the violinist I. V. Grzhimali and the cellist A. A. Brandukov, took part."

Here everything is correct except for one small error. The Principal of the School was not my father but Prince Lvov.

I remember very well the night described by Rodionov. I was awakened in the middle of it by a sweetly poignant pain, more violent than any I had ever experienced before. I cried out and burst into tears from fear and anguish. But the music drowned my cries and it was only after the movement of the trio that had awakened me had come to an end that I was heard. The curtain behind which I was lying and which divided the room into two was parted. My mother appeared, bent over me, and quickly calmed me. They must have taken me out to show to our visitors, or I may have seen our drawing room through the frame of the open door. It was full of tobacco smoke. The candles flickered, blinking like eyelashes, just as though the tobacco smoke had got into their eyes. They lit up brightly the polished red wood of the violin and cello. The grand piano loomed black. The frock coats of the men loomed black. The women emerged from dresses up to their shoulders, like birthday flowers out of flower baskets. The white hair of two or three old men blended with the rings of tobacco smoke. Afterwards I got to know one of them very well, and saw him often. It was the artist N. N. Ge. The image of the other passed through my whole

life, as through the life of most people, particularly
because my father illustrated his books, went to see
him, revered him, and because our whole house was
imbued with his spirit. It was Leo Nikolayevich
[Tolstoy]. . . .

Why then did I cry and why can I still remember
my suffering so clearly? I was accustomed to the
sound of the piano in the house; my mother played
it like a true artist. The voice of the grand piano
seemed to me an integral part of music itself. But the
timbres of stringed instruments, especially in their
chamber music ensemble, were foreign to me, and
they alarmed me like real cries for help and tidings
of disaster coming from outside through the small
ventilation window.

That, I believe, was the winter of two deaths: the
deaths of Anton Rubinstein and of Tchaikovsky.* I
suppose they must have been playing the famous
Tchaikovsky trio.†

That night stood like a landmark between the unconscious state of infancy and my subsequent childhood. With it my memory became active and my consciousness was set into motion, henceforward without
any great gaps and interruptions, as with grown-up
people.

* Actually, Tchaikovsky died in November, 1893, and Rubinstein in November, 1894.

† The trio "in memory of a great artist" (1881–82) composed
to commemorate the death of Nikolay Rubinstein.

In spring the shows of the Society for Travelling Art Exhibitions, the so-called *Peredvizhniki,* were held in the rooms of the Moscow Art School. The exhibition was usually brought from Petersburg in winter. The crates with the paintings were put in the sheds which stood in a line behind our house opposite our windows. Before Easter they were brought out into the yard and unpacked in the open before the doors of the sheds. The caretakers of the school opened the crates, unscrewed the pictures in their heavy frames from the top and bottom of the crates, and two men carried each picture across the yard to the exhibition. Perching on the window sills, we watched them eagerly. It was in this way that there passed before our eyes the most celebrated canvases of Repin, Myasoyedov, Makovsky, Surikov, and Polenov, a good half of the reserves of paintings of our present-day picture galleries and State storage depots.

The artists who were close to my father, as well as my father himself, exhibited at the travelling art shows only at the beginning and not for long. Soon Serov, Levitan, Korovin, Vrubel, Ivanov, my father, and others formed a new society, the Union of Russian Artists.

Toward the end of the nineties the sculptor Pavel Trubetskoy, who had spent all his life in Italy, arrived in Moscow. He was given a new studio with a glass roof. It was built against the wall of our house and one of its sides blocked up our kitchen window. Before, the window looked onto the garden, but now it faced Trubetskoy's sculpture studio. From the kitchen we watched his modelling and the work of his caster Robecchi as well as his models, including the small children and ballerinas who posed for him, and the carriages drawn by pairs of horses and the mounted Cossacks who rode in freely through the wide gates of the lofty studio.

It was from the same kitchen that my father's remarkable illustrations to Tolstoy's *Resurrection* were dispatched. After its final revision, the novel was serialized in the journal *Niva* by the Petersburg publisher Fyodor Marx. The work was feverish. I remember how pressed for time Father was. The issues of the journal came out regularly without delay. One had to be in time for each issue.

Tolstoy kept back the proofs, revising them again and again. There was the risk that the illustrations of the original text would be at variance with the corrections subsequently introduced into it. But my father's sketches came from the same source whence the author obtained his observations, the courtroom, the transit prison,* the country, the railway. It was the reservoir of living details, the identical realistic presentation of ideas, that saved him from the danger of digressing from the spirit of the original.

In view of the urgency of the matter, special precautions were taken to prevent any delay in the sending of the illustrations. The services of the conductors

* For prisoners going to Siberia.

of the express trains of the Nikolayevsky railway were enlisted. My childish imagination was struck by the sight of a train conductor in his formal railway uniform, standing waiting at the door of the kitchen as if he were standing on a railway platform at the door of the compartment of a train that was just about to leave the station.

Joiner's glue was boiling on the stove. The illustrations were hurriedly wiped dry, fixed, glued on pieces of cardboard, rolled up, tied up. The parcels, once ready, were sealed with sealing wax and handed to the conductor.

SCRIABIN

I

The first two decades of my life differ greatly from one another. In the nineties Moscow still preserved its old appearance of a fantastically picturesque provincial town with legendary features of the Third Rome or of the ancient capital city one reads about in the Russian epic poems, and with all the splendor of her famous "forty times forty" churches. Old customs were still observed. In the autumn, in Yushkov Lane, adjoining the yard of the School of Painting, in the yard of the Church of St. Florus and St. Laurus, who were regarded as the protectors of horse breeding, a service for the consecration of the horses took place, and the whole lane up to the gates of the school overflowed with horses and their drivers and stableboys, just as at a horse fair.

At the beginning of the new century everything was transformed in my memory as though by the wave of a magic wand. Moscow was seized by the business fever of the great capital cities. Big apartment houses were being rapidly put up with a view to getting larger returns on the invested capital. Brick giants, which seemed to grow imperceptibly, rose up to the very sky in all the streets. Together with them, Moscow, outstripping Petersburg, inaugurated a new Russian art, the art of a great city, a young, modern, new art.

2

The fever of the nineties had an effect on the School of Painting, too. The government grants were not sufficient for its maintenance. Businessmen were therefore entrusted with the raising of additional funds to cover its budget. It was decided to build on the land belonging to the school large apartment houses for letting to private persons, and to erect in the middle of the property, on the site of the former garden, glass exhibition galleries, also for letting. At the end of the 1890's began the work of pulling down the sheds and the cottages in the yard, and deep trenches were dug in the garden in place of its uprooted trees. The trenches became filled with water, and, as in ponds, drowned rats floated on the surface and frogs jumped and dived into them from the ground. Our house was also earmarked for demolition.

In winter a new apartment was fitted out for us in the main building of the school. It consisted of two or three classrooms and lecture rooms. We moved into it in 1901. As our new apartment, in which we spent ten years, had been made up of two large rooms one of which had been circular and the other of an even more fanciful form, our storeroom and bathroom were in the shape of a crescent, our kitchen was oval-shaped, and our dining room had a semicircular space cut out of it. Behind our front door we could always hear a subdued hubbub of voices from the corridors and the studios of the school, and from the last room on the other end we could hear the lectures on heating methods by Professor Chaplygin in the architecture class.

In the preceding years, in our old apartment, before I went to school, I was taught either by my mother or by some private tutor. At one time I was being prepared for entering the Petropavlovsk Grammar School and I studied all the subjects of the curriculum of the preparatory class in German.*

Of all these teachers, whom I remember with gratitude, I shall mention my first teacher, Yekaterina Ivanovna Baratynskaya, a writer of children's stories and a translator of children's books from the English. She taught me reading and writing, elementary arithmetic and French, starting from the very beginning, that is, how to sit on a chair and how to hold a pen in my hand. I was taken to her for my lessons in the furnished bed-sitting room she lived in. The room was dark. It was filled from top to bottom with books. It exuded an atmosphere of cleanliness and severity and it smelled of boiled milk and roasted coffee. On the other side of the window, covered with a lace curtain, grimy, grayish-cream flakes of snow were falling, looking like stitches of knitting. It distracted me and I did not give the right answers to Yekaterina Ivanovna,

* The Petropavlovsk school was attached to the Moscow Lutheran Church and was meant for the children of the German community, but it was popular also with many Russian families.

who was talking to me in French. At the end of the lesson, Yekaterina Ivanovna wiped my pen on the inside of her blouse, and, after waiting for those who were to take me home, dismissed me.

In 1901 I joined the second class of the Fifth Moscow Grammar School, which remained a classical school after Vannovsky's reforms, and which in addition to the several newly introduced subjects, including natural sciences, retained classical Greek in the curriculum.

3

In the spring of 1903 my father rented a house in the country at Obolenskoye, near Malo-Yaroslavets, on the Bryansk (now Kiev) railway line. Our country neighbor turned out to be Scriabin. At that time we had not yet become acquainted with the Scriabins.

Our country houses stood on a little hill along the edge of a wood at some distance from one another. We arrived in the country, as usual, in the early morning. The sunlight broke up into dancing fragments of light as it came through the foliage of the woodland trees that hung low over our house. The large bales of matting were being unpacked and ripped open. Bedding, provisions, pails, and frying pans were taken out of the bales. I ran off into the wood.

Dear Lord, what a morning! The things it was full of! The sunlight streamed through it in every direction; the moving shade of the trees kept setting its cap

Boris Pasternak at the age of eight, by Leonid Pasternak

now at one angle and now at another; on the upraised branches the birds burst into a chorus of chirping and twittering which always seems to be quite unexpected and which one can never get used to. It is loud and impetuous at first and dies down gradually, resembling in its passionate and repetitive persistence the trees of a thick forest that gradually fades away into the distance. And just as the light and shade followed upon each other in the forest and the birds sang and flew from one branch to another, so the passages and pieces of the Third Symphony or the *Divine Poem,* which was being composed on the piano in the country house next door, resounded and reverberated through it.

Lord, what music it was! The symphony was continually crumbling and tumbling like a city under artillery fire, and was all the time growing and being built up out of debris and wreckage. It was brimful of ideas minutely worked out to a point that was indistinguishable from frenzy, and at the same time as new as the forest, breathing life and freshness and, indeed, arrayed, surely, in the morning of the spring foliage of 1903 and not of 1803. And just as there was not a single leaf in that forest made of crimped paper or painted tin, so there was nothing in the symphony that was falsely profound or rhetorically respectable, "as in Beethoven," "as in Glinka," "like Ivan Ivanovich," "like Princess Maria Alexevna"; but the tragic force of the composition in the process of creation put out its tongue triumphantly at everything that was decrepit and generally accepted and majestically obtuse, and was bold to a point of frenzy, to a point of mischievousness, playfully elemental, and free like a fallen angel.

It might be thought that a man composing such music would understand what sort of man he was and, after his work, would be lucidly serene and restfully calm, like God resting from His labors on the seventh day. And so he was.

He often went for walks with my father on the Warsaw highway, which cut across the district. Sometimes I accompanied them. Having started to run, Scriabin loved to go on running and skipping as though with his own momentum, just like a stone rebounding on the surface of the water, just as though had he run a little faster he would have become detached from the earth and sailed in the air. In general, he cultivated various forms of inspired lightness and unencumbered motion on the borderline of flight. It is to a phenomenon of that kind that one has to attribute his charming elegance, the air of fine breeding with which he avoided appearing serious-minded in society and tried to seem lighthearted and superficial. All the more striking were his paradoxes during the country walks in Obolenskoye.

He argued with Father about life, about art, about good and evil, he attacked Tolstoy, preached the Superman, amorality, Nietzscheism. They agreed about

one thing—about the nature and the tasks of craftsmanship. About everything else they were poles apart.

I was twelve. Half of their arguments I did not
understand. But Scriabin won me by the freshness of
his spirit. I loved him to distraction. Without attempt-
ing to grasp the essence of his views, I was always on
his side. Soon he left for Switzerland, where he spent
six years.

That autumn our return to town was delayed because I had met with an accident. Father had planned
a painting, *Night Watch*. In it were depicted girls
from the village of Bocharovo who, riding at full speed
at sunset, were driving a drove of horses to the water
meadows at the bottom of our hill. One day I insisted on
accompanying him, and, as I took a jump over a wide
stream, I was thrown by my horse, which was tear-
ing along at breakneck speed, and broke a leg which
did not knit well, one of my legs remaining shorter
than the other, which later on exempted me from
military service at each draft.

Even earlier, before the summer in Obolenskoye, I
used to strum on the piano a little and made some
feeble attempts to compose something of my own.
Now, under the stimulus of my adoration of Scriabin,
the craving for improvisation and composition flared
up in me and grew into a passion. After that autumn
I devoted the following six years of my life, all the
years I spent at school, to a thorough study of the
theory of composition, first under the supervision of

the most excellent Y. D. Engel, a well-known mu-
sicologist and music critic of those days, and later
under the guidance of Professor R. M. Glier.

No one had any doubts about my future. My future
had been settled, my path in life correctly chosen. I
was meant to be a musician, everything was forgiven
me for the sake of music, every shape and form of in-
gratitude and rudeness toward my elders I was not
fit to hold a candle to, stubbornness, disobedience,
negligence, and strangeness of behavior. Even at school
when, during the Greek and math lessons, I was caught
trying to solve some fugue or counterpoint problem
and, asked to answer a question from my place, stood
like a fool and did not know what to say, my class-
mates did their best to shield me and my teachers for-
gave me everything. And in spite of that, I gave up
music.

I gave it up at a time when I had a right to be
pleased with myself, when everyone around was con-
gratulating me. My god and idol had returned from
Switzerland with *Ecstasy* and his last works. Moscow
celebrated his return and his victories. At the height of
his triumphs, I had the effrontery to go and see him
and play my compositions to him. His reception exceeded my expectations. Scriabin listened, encouraged,
inspired, blessed.

But no one knew of my secret trouble and, were I
to tell anyone about it, no one would have believed
me. While the advance I made as a composer was

pretty good, I was quite hopeless in a practical sense. I could scarcely play the piano and could not even read music with any fluency. I had to do it almost bar by bar. This discrepancy between the far from easy musical idea and its lagging technical support, transformed nature's gift, which could have served as a source of joy, into an object of constant torment which in the end I could no longer endure.

How was such a discrepancy possible? At its root lay something inadmissible, something that called for retribution, an unpardonable adolescent arrogance, a half-educated person's nihilistic disregard of everything that appears to him to be easily attainable and accessible. I despised everything uncreative, any kind of hack work, being conceited enough to imagine that I was a judge in these matters. In *real* life, I thought, everything must be a miracle, everything must be predestined from above, nothing must be deliberately designed or planned, nothing must be done to follow one's own fancies.

That was the negative side of Scriabin's influence, which in everything else became decisive for me. His egocentric nature was appropriate and justified only in his case. The seeds of his views, childishly misinterpreted, fell on favorable ground.

As it is, I was from early childhood inclined to mysticism and superstition and seized by a craving for the providential. Almost since the night described by Rodionov, I had believed in the existence of a higher heroic world, which must be served rapturously, though it might bring suffering. How many times at the age of six, seven, and eight was I near suicide!

I suspected all sorts of mysteries and deceptions around me. There was no absurdity in which I did not believe. At the dawn of life, when such idiocies are conceivable, perhaps because of the memories of the baby smocks in which I was arrayed still earlier, I imagined that at some time before I was born I had been a little girl and that I had to bring back that fascinating and delightful actuality by tightening my belt till I felt like fainting. And sometimes I imagined that I was not the son of my parents, but an adopted foundling.

In my misfortunes with music, too, it was the indirect, imaginary causes that were operative, such as belief in chance, expectation of signs and portents from above. I did not have perfect pitch; the faculty of recognizing the pitch of any arbitrarily taken note was an accomplishment that was absolutely unnecessary to me in my work. But the absence of this faculty depressed and humiliated me. I saw in it the proof that my music was against the will of fate and heaven. Under such a multitude of blows my spirits drooped and I lost heart.

Music, the beloved world of my labors, hopes, and anxieties for six years, I plucked out of myself and I parted from it as one parts from something most precious. For some time I kept up my improvisations on the piano from force of habit that was gradually growing weaker and weaker. But later on I decided to take stronger measures to enforce my abstinence. I stopped touching the piano, gave up going to concerts, and avoided meetings with musicians.

4

Scriabin's argument about the Superman was a characteristically Russian craving for the extraordinary. Actually, not only must music be supermusic to mean anything, but everything in the world must excel itself to be itself. Man, man's activity, must include an element of infinity which lends shape and style to a thing.

In view of my present backwardness so far as music is concerned and my atrophied and entirely extinct connections with it, all that is left of my memories of Scriabin, who meant so much to me and who was as important to me as my daily bread, is the Scriabin of the middle period, approximately from the Third to the Fifth Sonata.

The flashing harmonies of his *Prometheus* and his last works seem to me only the evidence of his genius and not daily food for the soul, and I am not in need of this evidence, because I believed in him without any proofs.

People on the verge of death, Andrey Bely, Khlebnikov, and some others, became absorbed before dying in the quest for new means of expression, in a pipe dream about a new language, they fumbled and rummaged about for its syllables, its vowels, and its consonants.

I could never understand those quests. In my opinion, the most striking discoveries are made when an artist is so full of his subject that it gives him no time to think about it and in his haste he proclaims his new word in the old language, without bothering his head as to whether it is new or old.

So, in the old language of Mozart and Field, Chopin said so much that was astonishingly new in music that it seemed to be its second beginning.

So Scriabin also, with the means that were at the disposal of his predecessors, renewed our sensation of music from its very foundation at the very beginning of his career. In the Studies of Opus 8 and in his Preludes of Opus 11, everything is already contemporary, everything is full of those inner correspondences, accessible to music, with the surrounding external world, with the way in which people of those days lived, thought, felt, travelled, and dressed.

No sooner do the melodies of those works begin than tears start to your eyes and they flow from the corners of your eyes along your cheeks down to the corners of your lips. The melodies, mingling with the tears, run straight along your nerves to your heart, and you weep not because you feel sad, but because the way to your heart has been found so unerringly and so shrewdly.

And all of a sudden in the course of the melody an answer or an objection to it bursts in in another voice, a higher and more feminine voice, in another and simpler conversational tone, an unexpected dispute, a discord that is instantly settled, and a note of a shattering naturalness is introduced into the work, the sort of naturalness that decides everything in a work of art.

Art is full of things that everyone knows about, of generally acknowledged truths. Although everyone is free to use them, the generally accepted principles have to wait a long time before they find an application. A generally acknowledged truth must wait for a rare piece of luck, a piece of luck that smiles upon it only once in a hundred years, before it can find any application. Such a piece of luck was Scriabin. Just as Dostoevsky is not only a novelist and just as Blok is not only a poet, so Scriabin is not only a composer, but an occasion for perpetual congratulations, a personified festival and triumph of Russian culture.

THE
NINETEEN
HUNDREDS

———

In response to the student demonstrations following
the manifesto of the 17th of October, [1905], the rabble
from Okhotny Ryad, the game market of Moscow,
got out of hand, and began to smash up the higher
educational institutions, the University and the Tech-
nological College. The School of Painting was also in
danger of being attacked. On the instructions of the
Principal of the School, heaps of cobblestones were
piled up on the landings of the main staircase and
hoses were screwed into the fire-cocks to repel any
attack by the looters.

Demonstrators turned in to the school from the
processions in the neighboring streets, held meetings
in the Assembly Hall, took possession of rooms, went
out on the balcony, and made speeches to those who
stayed in the streets below. The students of the school
formed militant organizations, and a fighting detach-
ment made up of them kept watch over the building
at night.

Among my father's papers are some sketches he
made at the time: a woman agitator, who was making
a speech on the balcony, is being shot at by dragoons
who swooped down on the crowd. She is wounded,
but she goes on with her speech, catching hold of a
column to prevent herself from falling.

47

At the end of 1905 Gorky arrived in Moscow, which was in the grip of a general strike. The nights were frosty. Plunged in darkness, Moscow was lit by bonfires. Stray bullets flew whistling through the streets and mounted patrols galloped wildly over the noiseless, virginal snow, untrampled by pedestrians.

Father saw Gorky in connection with the political, satirical journals *The Whip, The Bugbear,* and others, whenever the latter invited him to their editorial offices.

I expect it must have been just then or later, after I had spent a year in Berlin with my parents, that I saw Blok's poems for the first time in my life. I cannot remember whether it was *Pussywillows* or some of his *Childhood Poems,* dedicated to Olenina d'Alheim, or something revolutionary, something about the city, but my impression I remember so distinctly that I can re-create it and I am going to attempt to describe it.

2

What is literature in the generally accepted and most widely understood meaning of the word? It is a world of eloquence, platitudes, rounded sentences, and venerable names of people who, when young, had observed life and who, on becoming famous, had passed on to abstractions, reiterations, and ratiocinations. And when in this realm of accepted, and only because of that unnoticed, artificiality, someone opens his mouth, not because of any inherent bent for literature, but because he knows something and wants to say it, this creates the impression of a revolution, just as though a door were flung open and the noise of the life going on outside came through it, just as though it were not a man explaining what was going on in the town, but the town itself announcing its presence through the lips of a man. So it was with Blok. Such was his solitary, unspoilt, childlike word, such was the powerful effect it produced.

A piece of paper contained a certain amount of information. It seemed as though the information had itself, without being asked, settled down on the sheet of printed paper, as though no one had composed and written the poem. It seemed as though the page were covered not with verses about wind and puddles, street lamps and stars, but the street lamps and the puddles themselves were spreading their wind-blown ripples on the surface of the journal, as though they themselves had left the damp imprints that exerted so powerful an influence on the reader.

3

A number of writers of my age as well as myself went through the years of our youth with Blok as our guide. Blok had everything that goes to make a great poet: fire, tenderness, emotion, his own image of the world, his own special gift for transforming everything he touched, and his own restrained, hidden, self-absorbed destiny. Of all these qualities and many more, I shall pause to consider only one side of his genius that has, perhaps, left the deepest impression on me and for that reason seems to me to be the most important one, namely Blok's impetuosity, his roving intentness, the rapidity of his observations.

> *A gleam in the window,*
> *A porch without light;*
> *A Harlequin whispers*
> *Alone with the night.*
>
> *The snow in the streets is whirled and tossed*
> *Round and round in faltering dance,*
> *And here a hand is offered me,*
> *And there a smile in someone's glance.*
>
> *And there with a light one teases and flashes,*
> *So often in winter night disguises*
> *A shade, a shape that now appears*
> *But soon departs and wholly vanishes.*

Adjectives without nouns, predicates without subjects, hide-and-seek, breathless agitation, nimbly darting little figures, abruptness—how that style seemed to agree with the spirit of the age, hiding, secretive, underground, barely emerged from the cellars, talking in the language of conspirators, of which the chief character was the city and the chief event the street.

These features permeate Blok's entire being, the fundamental and the predominant Blok, the Blok of the second volume of the Alkonost edition, the Blok of *The Terrible World, The Last Day, The Deception, Story, The Legends, The Political Meeting, The Stranger,* the poems: *In the Mists Above the Sparkling Dew, In the Pubs, Lanes and Winding Streets,* and *A Girl Sang in the Church Choir.*

The features of reality are brought into Blok's books like currents of air by the whirlwind of his sensibility. Even the most remote, which might appear to be mystical and might even be called "divine," that, too, is not a metaphysical fantasy but bits of reality culled from ecclesiastical life and scattered through all his poems, pieces out of the Greek Orthodox service, prayers before communion, and requiem psalms, known by heart and heard a thousand times during church services.

The sum total of this world, the bearer of this reality, was the city of Blok's poems, the chief hero of his *Story* and of his biography.

This city, this Petersburg of Blok's, is the most real of Petersburgs depicted by the artists of most recent times. It exists alike in life and imagination without any difference whatever. It is full of that everyday prose which feeds poetry with its drama and its anxieties, and in its streets resounds the everyday colloquial speech which is in general use and which enlivens the language of poetry.

At the same time the image of that city is composed of features selected by a hand so sensitive and is subjected to such inspired treatment, that it has all been transmuted into the most thrilling phenomenon of the rarest inner world.

4

I have had the occasion and the good luck to know many older poets who lived in Moscow: Bryusov, Andrey Bely, Khodasevich, Vyacheslav Ivanov, Baltrushaitis. I introduced myself to Blok for the first time during his last visit to Moscow,* in the corridor or on the staircase of the Polytechnic Museum on the evening of his address in the lecture theater of the Museum. Blok was nice to me, he said he had heard many good things about me, he complained of not feeling well and asked me to postpone my visit to him till he felt better.

That evening he read his poems in three places: at the Polytechnic Museum, at the Press Club, and at the Society of Dante Alighieri, where the most zealous of his admirers had gathered and where he read his *Italian Poems.*

Mayakovsky was present at the Polytechnic Museum. In the middle of the reading he told me that an anti-Blok demonstration was being organized at the Press Club under the pretext of critical integrity, and that

* Blok arrived in Moscow on May 1, 1921. During his visit he gave six readings of his poetry. He died on August 7th in Petersburg.

at that "benefit" performance Blok would be booed and shouted down. He suggested that the two of us should go there and try to prevent that contemptible attack planned by Blok's enemies.

We left the Blok meeting and walked to the Press Club. But Blok was taken to his second meeting by car, and by the time we made our way to the Nikitsky Boulevard, where the Press Club was, the reading was over and Blok had gone to the Society of friends of Italian literature. The hostile demonstration which we feared had in the meantime taken place. After his reading at the Press Club, Blok had been told a lot of monstrous things; some of his attackers were not even ashamed to tell him to his face that he was out of date and had been dead without realizing it for many years, with which he calmly agreed. That was said to him only a few months before his real death.

5

In those years of our first attempts to challenge the accepted conventions of poetic expression only two poets, Aseyev and Marina Tsvetayeva, possessed the mastery over a mature and completely formed poetic style. The acclaimed originality of the others, including my own, arose from our utter helplessness and in-articulateness, which did not, however, prevent us from writing, publishing, and translating. Among my depressingly incompetent writings of that time, the most

awful ones were my translations of Ben Jonson's
Alchemist and Goethe's poem *The Mysteries.* There
is extant a review of them by Blok published in the
last volume of his collected works among his other
reviews written for the publishing house World Literature. This scornful and scathing criticism is well de-
served and justified in its final appraisal.

However, from all these digressions it is time we
returned to our story, which we interrupted at the
years long since passed, the early nineteen hundreds.

6

When a schoolboy in the third or fourth class, I
travelled by myself to Petersburg for the Christmas
vacation on a free ticket given me by my uncle, the
stationmaster of the Petersburg freight station of the
Nikolayevsky line. For days on end I wandered about
the streets of the immortal city, as though devouring
with my feet and eyes a sort of magnificent stone book,
and the evenings I spent at Kommissarzhevskaya's
theater. I was intoxicated with the newest literature,
raved about Andrey Bely, Hamsun, Przybyszewski.

A still greater and more real idea of travel I got
from the trip of our whole family to Berlin in 1906.
This was the first time that I found myself abroad.
Everything was unusual, everything different. I felt
as though I were not awake, but dreaming, taking
part in some imaginary theatrical performance which

no one was really obliged to take part in. You don't know anyone, no one can lay down the law for you. A long row of slamming and opening doors along the entire wall of the railway carriage, a separate door for each compartment. Four tracks on the elevated belt railway, suspended over the streets, canals, race-horse stables, and the back yards of the gigantic city. Trains overtaking other trains, driving alongside or crossing the paths of other trains. A double line of street lights, crisscrossing and intersecting lights under the bridges, lights in the second and third floors of houses level with the overhead railway lines, the multicolored lights of the automatic machines in the station buffets, ejecting cigars, sweets, sugared almonds. I soon got used to Berlin, loafed about its numberless streets and immense park, spoke German, tried to imitate the Berlin dialect, breathed a mixture of locomotive smoke, coal gas, and beer foam, listened to Wagner.

Berlin was full of Russians. The composer Rebikov played his *Christmas Tree* to his friends and divided music into three periods: animal music before Beethoven, human music during the next period, and the music of the future after himself.

Gorky, too, was in Berlin. Father made a drawing of him. Andreyeva objected to the cheekbones on the drawing's being so prominent that they looked angular. She said: "You haven't understood him. He is Gothic." That was how most people talked in those days.

7

It was, I think, after this trip abroad, on my return to Moscow, that another great lyric poet of the century entered into my life, a lyric poet who was scarcely known at the time, but who has now been acknowledged by the entire world: the German poet, Rainer Maria Rilke.

In 1900 he went to see Tolstoy in Yasnaya Polyana; he knew my father and corresponded with him. One summer he spent with the peasant poet Drozhzhin in Zavidovo, near Klin.

In those far-off days, he used to present his early collections of poems to Father with warm inscriptions. Two of these books fell into my hands rather late during one of the winters I have described, and I was struck by the same things that amazed me in the first poems of Blok I ever saw: the urgency of what they had to say, the absoluteness, the gravity, the direct purposefulness of their language.

8

Rilke is entirely unknown in Russia. The few attempts to render him into Russian have not been successful. The translators are not to blame. They are accustomed to translate the meaning and not the tone of a poem, and with Rilke the tone is everything.

In 1913 Verhaeren was in Moscow. Father painted his portrait. A few times Father asked me to keep the poet entertained so as to prevent his face from growing stiff and lifeless. Once I had diverted the historian V. O. Klyuchevsky in this way. Now came my turn to divert Verhaeren. With understandable enthusiasm I told him how I admired his poetry and then I asked him timidly if he had heard of Rilke. I never thought that Verhaeren would know him. The poet looked transformed. Father could not have asked for anything better. The name of Rilke alone revived his model more than any of my conversations. "He is the best European poet," said Verhaeren, "and my favorite spiritual brother."

With Blok prose remains the source of the poem. It does not form any part of his means of expression. With Rilke the true-to-life and psychological methods of our contemporary novelists (Tolstoy, Flaubert, Proust, and the Scandinavians) are inseparable from the style and the language of his poetry.

9

Somewhere about the beginning of 1907 new publishing houses began popping out of the ground like mushrooms, concerts of new music were given much oftener than before, one after another there opened exhibitions of pictures by painters belonging to different groups, such as the World of Art, the Golden

Fleece, the Jack of Diamonds, the Donkey's Tail, and the Blue Rose. Beside the Russian names of Somov, Sapunov, Sudeikin, Krymov, Larionov, and Goncharova there appeared the names of Bonnard and Vuillard. At the exhibitions of the Golden Fleece, in rooms shaded by curtains, where, as in hothouses, it smelled of earth from the flowerpots of hyacinths, one could see the works of Rodin and Matisse. The young people joined these movements.

In the courtyard of one of the new houses in Razgulyay Square was preserved an old wooden cottage belonging to the general who owned the house. The general's son, the poet and artist Julian Pavlovich Anissimov, used to hold parties in the attic of the cottage for young people who held the same views as he. He had weak lungs. He spent the winters abroad. His friends gathered at his place when the weather was good in spring and autumn. They read, made music, painted, talked, ate snacks, and drank tea with rum. There I made the acquaintance of a large number of people.

Our host, a highly talented man of excellent taste, who spoke several foreign languages as fluently as he did Russian, was himself an embodiment of poetry, but as he was only an amateur of great charm it was rather difficult for him to be, in addition, a strong creative personality, a character out of which a master of his craft is eventually produced. We had similar interests, we admired the same people. I liked him very much.

The late Sergey Nikolayevich Durylin, who at that time used to write under the pseudonym of Sergey Rayevsky, used to go there. It was he who persuaded me to give up music in favor of literature and who, out of the kindness of his heart, was able to find something worthy of attention in my first literary efforts. He was poor, keeping his mother and his aunt on what he earned from private lessons, and by his enthusiastic candor and furious conviction of the rightness of his ideas reminded me of Belinsky as tradition paints him.

It was there that my university colleague K. G. Loks, whom I had known before, showed me for the first time the poems of Innokenty Annensky, because he seemed to find a certain kinship between my writings and ramblings and the work of the remarkable poet who was quite unknown to me at the time.

This circle of friends had its own name. It was christened Serdarda, a name whose meaning no one knew. This word was said to have been heard one day on the Volga by a member of our circle, the poet and bass Arkady Guryev. He had heard it at night during a commotion on the quay created by two river steamers after one of them had made fast to the other and the passengers of the second steamer had disembarked with their baggage by walking through the saloon of the first steamer, which had made fast to the quay earlier, and mingled with her passengers and their baggage.

Guryev was a native of Saratov. He had a powerful

and soft voice and he gave highly artistic renderings of the dramatic and vocal subtleties of whatever he happened to be singing. Like all born but untrained artists, he struck you equally by his perpetual buffoonery and the rudiments of genuine originality which one glimpsed through his affectation. His far from mediocre poems anticipated the future unrestrained candor of Mayakovsky and the clear-cut images of Esenin so easily grasped by the reader. He was a natural operatic and dramatic actor, the sort of born actor who was more than once depicted by Ostrovsky.

His head was rounded like an onion, his forehead was large, his nose barely perceptible, and there were unmistakable signs that he would end up with a skull as bare as the back of his hand. He was all movement, expressiveness. He did not gesticulate or wave his arms about, but when he engaged in arguments or recited, though he might be standing still, the upper part of his body seemed to be walking, acting, and talking. He inclined his head, threw back his body, and put his feet far apart as though caught tapping his heels in the middle of a folk dance. He was a little given to drink and when drunk believed in his own inventions. At the end of his turns he pretended that his heel had stuck to the floor and he could not tear it away, and he assured his audience that the devil was trying to catch him by the foot.

There were poets and artists in Serdarda: B. B. Krasin, who set Blok's *Pussywillows* to music, Sergey

Bobrov, the future partner of my early debuts, whose appearances in Razgulyay Square were preceded by rumors that he was a newly arisen Russian Rimbaud, A. I. Kozhebatkin, editor of *Musaget,* and Sergey Makovsky, editor of *Apollon,* whenever he was on a visit to Moscow.

I myself joined Serdarda on the strength of my standing as a musician and improvised on the piano a musical description of every new arrival at the beginning of the evening.

The short spring nights passed quickly. The cold morning breeze wafted through the open window. It raised the skirts of the curtains, stirred the flames of the guttering candles, rustled the sheets of paper on the table. And everyone—the guests and our host—was yawning. Empty vistas, a gray sky, rooms, staircases. We each went our way, overtaking in the wide streets, which seemed to go on forever because of the absence of people, the interminable lines of the rumbling night carts of the Public Health Department. "Centaurs," someone remarked in the language of the period.

10

Around the *Musaget* publishing house there was formed something in the nature of an academy. Andrey Bely, Stepun, Rachinsky, Boris Sadovsky, Emile Metner, Shenrok, Petrovsky, Ellis, and Nilender taught the young people who were interested in the subjects of poetic rhythm, the history of the German romantic movement, Russian lyric poetry, the aesthetics of Goethe and Richard Wagner, Baudelaire and the French symbolists, and ancient Greek pre-Socratic philosophy.

The mind behind all these undertakings was Andrey Bely, the unchallenged authority of that circle in those days, a first-class poet and author of the particularly striking *Symphonies in Prose* and of the novels *The Silver Dove* and *Petersburg,* which created an upheaval in the pre-Revolutionary taste of his contemporaries and gave rise to the first Soviet prose.

Andrey Bely possessed all the marks of genius that refused to be driven into a rut by the petty worries of everyday life, by family, by the lack of understanding of those near and dear to him, a genius that ran amok and from a productive force was transformed into a destructive and barren one. This flaw of superabundant inspiration did not discredit him, but aroused one's sympathy and added a martyrlike touch to his charm.

He gave lectures on the practical study of the Russian classical iambic verse and by the method of statistical calculation analyzed, together with his students, its rhythmic figures and variations. I did not go to his lectures because I have been, and am now too, of the opinion that the music of the word is not an acoustic phenomenon and does not consist of the euphony of vowels and consonants, taken by themselves, but of the relationship between the meaning and the sound of the words.

The young people did not always meet in the offices of *Musaget,* but in all sorts of other places. Such a meeting place was the studio of the sculptor Kracht in the Presnya section.

The studio had a living space on top in the form of an enclosed gallery high up near the ceiling; below, dressed in ivy leaves and other decorative greenery, were the white casts of fragments of antique sculpture, plaster-of-Paris masks, and the original works of the owner of the studio.

One day in late autumn I read in this studio a paper under the title of "Symbolism and Immortality." Part of my audience was sitting below and another part was listening above, lying on the floor of the gallery with their heads sticking out over its edge.

My paper was based on the idea that our perceptions are subjective, on the fact that the sounds and colors we perceive in nature correspond to something else, namely to the objective vibrations of the sound and light waves. In my paper I argued that this subjectivity was not the attribute of every individual human being, but was a generic and suprapersonal quality, that it was the subjectivity of the world of man and of humanity at large. I suggested in my paper that after his death every person leaves behind him a part of that undying, generic subjectivity which he possessed during his lifetime and with which he participated in the history of mankind's existence. The main object of my paper was to advance the theory that perhaps this preeminently subjective and universally human corner or separate part of the soul had since time immemorial been the sphere of action and the main subject of art. That, besides, though the artist was of course mortal like the rest of mankind, the joy of living experienced by him was immortal, and that other people a century later might through his works be able to experience something approaching the personal and vital form of his original sensations.

My paper was entitled "Symbolism and Immortality" because in it I affirmed the symbolic, conventional quiddity of every art in the general sense in which one can talk of the symbolism of algebra.

My paper created a stir. It was talked about. I came back home late. At home I learned that Tolstoy, stopped by illness after his flight from Yasnaya Polyana, had died at the railway station of Astapovo and that Father had been summoned there by telegram. We packed our things quickly and drove to Paveletsky Station to catch the night train.*

II

At that time one noticed the departure from town more than now. The landscape of the countryside looked more different from the urban landscape than

* Tolstoy left Yasnaya Polyana on the early morning of November 10, 1910. He travelled third-class by train. He caught a chill and died of pneumonia in the stationmaster's house at Astapovo on November 20.

at the present time. From the morning, and for the rest of the day, the window of our compartment was filled with the vast expanse of fields, some fallow and some under winter corn, enlivened only by a glimpse of an occasional village, the vast, thousand-mile expanse of arable Russia, the Russia of peasant villages, which feed the small area of urban Russia and work for it. The first frosts had already silvered the earth and the gold that still hung on the birch trees framed it all along the boundaries of the fields, and this silver of the frosts and the gold of the birch trees lay on her like a modest ornament, like gold leaf and silver foil on her sacred and meek antiquities.

The plowed and fallow land that flashed by in the windows of the carriage was not conscious that somewhere close by, somewhere not very far away, her last giant lay dead, a man who because of his high birth could have been her Tsar, and because of the richness of his intellect, saturated with all the subtleties of the world, could have been the greatest darling and the grandest gentleman of them all. But out of love for her and out of a sense of justice toward her he walked behind the plow and dressed and girt himself with a belt like a peasant.

12

I expect it must have become known that artists would make drawings of the deceased and that afterwards a caster, who had arrived with Merkurov, would take his death mask, for those who had come to bid a last farewell were asked to leave the room. When we entered it, it was empty. Sofia Andreyevna, with a tear-stained face, stepped forward rapidly from a far corner of the room and, seizing my father's hands, cried spasmodically in a voice choked with tears: "Oh, Leonid Osipovich, you can't imagine what I've been through! You, at least, know how much I loved him!" And she began telling him how after Tolstoy had left she had tried to commit suicide by throwing herself into a pond and how she had been dragged out of it more dead than alive.

In the room lay a mountain like Elbrus, and she was one of its large, detached crags; the room was filled by a storm cloud the size of half the sky, and she was one of its separate lightnings. And she did not realize that she had the privilege of a crag and of a sheet of lightning to be silent and to crush by the mysteriousness of her conduct; that she need not enter into arguments with those who were the most un-Tolstoyan in the world—the Tolstoyans; that she need not join in a pygmy battle with those people.

But she tried to justify herself and appealed to my father to be a witness that she excelled her rivals in her devotion and her intellectual understanding, and that she would have taken care of her late husband better than they. Good Lord, I thought, to what a state can a human being be reduced, and a wife of Tolstoy, at that!

It is, in fact, strange. A modern man who rejects the duel as an outworn convention writes an enormous work on the subject of Pushkin's duel and Pushkin's death. Poor Pushkin! He should have married Shchegolev and the latest Pushkiniana and everything would have been perfect! He would have lived to our own days and would have composed several continuations of *Eugene Onegin* and written five Poltava poems instead of one. And yet, it always seemed to me that I would have ceased to understand Pushkin if I were to admit that he was more in need of our understanding than of Natalya Nikolayevna.

13

It was not, however, a mountain that lay in the corner of the room, but a little, wizened old man, one of the old men created by Tolstoy, one of those he had described and scattered over his pages by the dozen. Little Christmas trees stood all around the place. The setting sun cut across the room with four slanting shafts of light and formed a cross over the corner where the body was lying with the thick shadow of the window-bars and other little baby crosses with the traceries of the young Christmas trees.

The railway hamlet of Astapovo was transformed that day into a discordantly noisy encampment of world journalism. The station buffet did a roaring trade, the waiters were run off their feet, too busy to carry out all the orders of their customers and serving underdone beefsteaks at a run. Rivers of beer were consumed.

Tolstoy's sons Ilya and Andrey were at the station. His other son Sergey arrived by the train which had come to take Tolstoy's remains to Yasnaya Polyana.

To the chanting of a requiem, the students and the young people carried the coffin across the little yard and the garden of the stationmaster's house to the railway platform and put it in the freight car, and to the accompaniment of the resumed singing, the train slowly moved off in the direction of Tula.

It seemed natural, somehow, that Tolstoy was at peace and that he should have found peace by the wayside like a pilgrim, near the main lines of communication of the Russia of those days, which his heroes and heroines continued to fly past and pass and repass, looking through the windows of the train at the insignificant railway station they were passing through, without realizing that the eyes which had watched them all their lives, the eyes which had seen through them and immortalized them, had closed forever in it.

14

If we were to take only one quality from every writer—for instance, if we were to characterize Lermontov by passionateness, Tyutchev by the richness of his subject matter, Chekhov by his poetic qualities,

Gogol by his dazzling brilliance, Dostoevsky by his imaginative powers—what are we to say of Tolstoy, if we must limit the definition to one characteristic only?

The chief quality of this moralist, leveller, and preacher of a system of justice that would embrace everybody without fear or favor would be an originality that distinguished him from everyone else and that verged on the paradoxical.

All his life and at any given moment he possessed the faculty of seeing things in the detached finality of each separate moment, in sharp relief, as we see things only on rare occasions, in childhood, or on the crest of an all-embracing happiness, or in the triumph of a great spiritual victory.

To see things like that it is necessary that one's eye should be directed by passion. For it is passion that by its flash illuminates an object, intensifying its appearance.

Such a passion, the passion of creative contemplation, Tolstoy constantly carried about within himself. Indeed, it was in its light that he saw everything in its pristine freshness, in a new way, as though for the first time. The authenticity of what he saw differs so much from what we are used to that it may appear strange to us. But Tolstoy was not looking for this strangeness, he was not pursuing it as an aim in itself, and he most certainly did not use it in his works as a literary method.

Boris Pasternak,
by L. Pasternak

BEFORE THE
FIRST WORLD WAR

———

During the first half of 1912, the spring and summer, I lived abroad. Our school vacations coincide with the summer semester of the West. This semester I spent in the old University of Marburg.

It was at this university that Lomonosov often attended the lectures of the mathematician and philosopher Christian Wolff. A century and a half before him, Giordano Bruno had read the essay on his new astronomy there before his return from his foreign tour to Italy and his death at the stake in Rome.

Marburg is a small medieval town. In those days it numbered twenty-nine thousand inhabitants. Half of these were students. It clings picturesquely to the side of a mountain, from which are quarried the stones that were used for the building of its houses, churches, castles, and university, and it is buried in dense orchards, dark as the night.

Of the money that had been assigned for my living expenses and studies in Germany, I had only a little left over. On this unspent remainder of my funds I went to Italy. I saw Venice, brick-pink and aquamarine-green, like the transparent pebbles which the sea casts ashore, and I paid a visit to Florence, dark, narrow, slender—a living extraction from Dante's tercets. I had no money left for a sight-seeing tour of Rome.

The following year I completed my course at Moscow University. I was assisted in passing my examinations by Mansurov, a young postgraduate research student in history. He supplied me with a whole collection of textbooks and lecture notes which he had used himself before passing his finals the year before. The professorial library greatly exceeded the examination requirements, and in addition to general textbooks it contained reference books on classical antiquities and separate monographs on all sorts of subjects. It was with difficulty that I took away all those riches in a cab.

Mansurov was a relative and a friend of the young Trubetskoy and Dmitry Samarin. I knew them from the Fifth Grammar School, where they used to pass their examinations every year after having been taught at home.

The elder Trubetskoys, the father and uncle of the student Nikolay, were one a professor of jurisprudence, and the other Rector of the University and a well-known philosopher. Both were notable for their vast corpulence and, elephants in frock coats without waists, used to clamber up to the rostrum in the lecture hall and read their remarkable lectures in whining, beseeching, muffled, aristocratically burring voices.

The three inseparable young men, who used always to drop in at the university together, were of the same breed: tall, gifted youths with eyebrows growing right across their foreheads and with high-sounding voices and names.

The Marburg school of philosophy was held in high honor in that circle. Trubetskoy wrote about it and sent his more gifted students there to perfect themselves. Dmitry Samarin, who had been there before me, was quite at home there. He was a zealot of Marburg. I went there on his advice.

Dmitry Samarin belonged to a famous Slavophile family, on whose former estate there is now situated the writers' village of Peredelkino and the Peredelkino Tuberculosis Sanatorium for Children.

Philosophy, dialectics, and a knowledge of Hegel were in his blood. He had inherited it. He was untidy, absent-minded, and possibly not quite normal. As a result of his strange behavior when his fits came over him he was very difficult to live with and quite unbearable in society. It is impossible to blame his family, who could not get on with him and with whom he was constantly quarrelling.

At the beginning of NEP he returned to Moscow from Siberia, where he had spent a long time carried hither and thither during the Civil War. He had grown much more simple and more understanding. He had swollen up from starvation and become covered with lice during his journey. He fell ill with typhus, at a time when the epidemic was on the wane, and died.

I do not know what became of Mansurov, but the famous philosopher Nikolay Trubetskoy became a world celebrity and died in Vienna a short time ago.

2

The summer after my finals I spent with my parents at their country house at Molodya near the Stolbovaya railway station on the Moscow-Kursk line.

From our house, according to tradition, the Cossacks of our retreating army returned the fire of the advancing forward detachments of Napoleon's troops. On the grounds, which merged with the adjoining cemetery, their graves were sunk and overgrown.

Inside the house the rooms were narrow in proportion to their high ceilings and high windows. The oil lamp on the table threw immense shadows in the corners of the dark red walls and on the ceiling.

At the bottom of the park meandered a little stream with many deep eddies. A large old birch tree, half broken, continued to grow lopsidedly over one of the eddies. The green tangle of its branches formed an overhead summerhouse. It was quite safe to make oneself comfortable in their strong interlacement either by sitting or half lying down. Here I made myself a place to work in.

I read Tyutchev and for the first time in my life wrote poetry not as a rare exception, but often and continuously, as one paints or composes music.

In the thicket of that tree I wrote the poems of my first book in two or three summer months.

The book was, with quite stupid pretentiousness, en-

titled *A Twin in the Clouds,* in imitation of the cosmo-
logical ingenuities which were characteristic of the
book titles of the symbolists and the names of their
publishing houses.

To write those poems, to cross out, revise, and correct them and then rewrite them again, was something
that I felt to be an absolute necessity and gave me immense pleasure that brought me to the verge of tears.

I did my best to avoid any romantic affectation, any
attempt to engage the interest of the reader by something that was not germane to the main theme of the
poem. I had no desire to declaim these poems from the
stage at the top of my voice so that people engaged in
intellectual pursuits should shy away from them, cry-
ing indignantly: "What degradation! What barbarity!"
I did not want flies and wives of professors to expire
because of their discreet elegance, or that after reading
them to a small audience of six or seven admirers I
should be told: "Permit me to shake hands with an
honest man!" I was not trying to achieve the clear-cut
rhythms of a song or a dance, under whose influence
almost without the participation of words hands and
feet begin to move by themselves. I did not express, re-
flect, represent, or depict anything at all.

Later on, as a result of quite unnecessary attempts to
find some sort of affinity between Mayakovsky and myself, people discovered oratorical and melodic tendencies
in my poems. This is not correct. They are there no
more than in the speech of any ordinary person.

Quite the contrary, the subject matter of my poems was my constant preoccupation, my constant dream was that my poem itself should have something in it, that it should have a new idea or a new picture, that it should be engraved with all its peculiarities in the book and should speak from its pages with all its silence and with all the colors of its black colorless print.

For instance, I wrote a poem *Venice* and a poem *The Railway Station*. The city on the water stood before me and the circles and figures of eight of its reflections widened and multiplied, swelling like a rusk in tea. Or, far away, at the end of the tracks and platforms, there arose before me, all in clouds and smoke, a railway farewell horizon, behind which the trains were hidden, and which contained the history of relationships, meetings and partings, and the events before and after them.

There was nothing I demanded from myself, from my readers, or from the theory of art. All I wanted was that one poem should contain the city of Venice and the other the Brest (now the Belorussko-Baltiysky) railway station.

Bobrov liked the lines, "Sometimes the West moved apart in shuntings of trains and sleepers" from my *Railway Station*. Aseyev and I, together with a few other young writers, founded a small co-operative publishing house by pooling all our available resources. Bobrov, who knew all there was to know about typography from his work at the *Russian Archives,* published his own things with our publishing house and edited our things for it. He published the *Twin* with a friendly preface by Aseyev.

Maria Ivanovna Baltrushaitis, the wife of the poet, used to say: "One day you will be sorry to have published an immature book." She was right. I was often sorry to have done so.

3

I spent the hot summer of 1914 with its drought and full eclipse of the sun at the country cottage of the Baltrushaitises on a large estate on the Oka near the town of Alexin. I was their son's tutor and I was also translating Kleist's comedy *The Broken Jug* for the newly founded Kamerny Theater, of which Baltrushaitis was the literary director.

There were many people from the world of art on the estate, such as Vyacheslav Ivanov, the artist Ulyanov, and the wife of the writer Muratov. Not far away, in Tarussa, Balmont was translating *Sakuntala* by Kalidasa for the same theater. In July I was called up and went to Moscow for my medical and obtained a "white ticket," that is to say, complete exemption from military service because of my shortened leg which I had broken as a boy. I then returned to the Baltrushaitises' summer place on the Oka.

Shortly after that, something of this sort happened one evening. From behind a curtain of mist that hung over the rushes in the river Oka, the strains of a military band playing some sort of regimental music, a polka or a march, were slowly floating toward us from below and coming nearer and nearer. Then a little tug with three barges in tow appeared from behind a promontory. They must have sighted the estate on the top of the hill from the tug and decided to land. The tug sailed straight across the river and brought the barges to our bank. There were soldiers on them, a large unit of a grenadier regiment. They disembarked and lit campfires at the foot of the hill. The officers were invited to the house to dine and spend the night there. In the morning they sailed away. It was one of the episodes of the general mobilization. The war began.

4

Then I spent about a year, in two separate stages with a few breaks between them, in the family of a rich businessman, Moritz Philippe, as tutor of their son Walter, a nice and affectionate boy.

During the anti-German riots in the summer, Philippe's offices and private house were looted together with the biggest private firms, such as Einem and Verrein. The destruction was proceeding according to plan and with the knowledge of the police. The property belonging to the employees was not touched, only the things belonging to the owners of the German firms. In the ensuing confusion my linen, clothes, and other things were saved, but my books and manuscripts were destroyed in the general turmoil.

Later on, many of the things I had written got lost under more peaceful conditions. I do not like my style up to 1940, I reject half of Mayakovsky, and I do not like everything of Esenin's. The general disintegration of form in those days, the impoverishment of thought, the uneven and impure style are foreign to me. I am not worried about the disappearance of imperfect and faulty works. But neither was I ever sorry for the loss of successful works, though for quite a different reason.

In life it is more necessary to lose than to gain. A seed will only germinate if it dies. One has to live without getting tired, one must look forward and feed on one's living reserves, which oblivion no less than memory produces.

At different times I have lost for different reasons: the text of my paper "Symbolism and Immortality," the articles of my futuristic period, a fairy tale for children in prose, two poems, a notebook of verses, intermediate between *Above the Barriers* and *My Sister, Life,* the rough copy of a novel in several foolscap notebooks, the revised beginning of which was published as a long short story under the title *The Childhood of Luverse,* and, finally, my translation of one whole tragedy from Swinburne's dramatic trilogy on Mary Stuart.

We moved to a new rented apartment from Philippe's looted and half-burnt house. There I had a room to myself. I remember it very well. The rays of the setting autumn sun furrowed the room and the book I was looking through. There were two kinds of evening in the book. One lay across it with a light rosy hue. The other was made up of the contents and the soul of the poems published in it.

I envied its author, who was able to retain the bits of reality she had put into it with such simple means. It was one of Akhmatova's first books, probably *The Plantain*.

5

During the same years, in the intervals between my work at the Philippes', I travelled to the Urals and the Kama district. One winter I lived in Vsevolodo-Vilva in the north of the province of Perm, which, according to the reminiscences of A. N. Tikhonov, who described those places, Chekhov and Levitan had once upon a time visited. Another winter I spent in the Quiet Mountains on the Kama River at the chemical works of the Ushkovs.

In the offices of the works, I was for some time in charge of the draft board and freed whole districts of people attached to factories and doing defense work from military service.

In winter the factories kept in communication with

Anna Akhmatova, by G. Annenkov

the outside world by antediluvian methods. The mail came by sledges drawn by teams of three horses from Kazan, about two hundred miles away, as in the days of Pushkin's *Captain's Daughter*. Once I took part in this winter journey.

When, in March, 1917, the news that the Revolution had broken out in Petersburg reached the factories, I left for Moscow.

At the Izhev factory I had to find and take with me a remarkable man, an engineer by the name of Zbarsky, who had been sent there on a special mission. I had to put myself under his orders and go with him.

From the Quiet Mountains we travelled in a *kibitka*, a covered cart on runners, a whole night and part of the following day. Wrapped in three long peasant overcoats and buried in hay, I rolled round and round like a big, heavy sack on the bottom of the sledge, bereft of all freedom of movement. I dozed, nodded, fell asleep and woke up, closed and opened my eyes.

I saw the road through the forest, the stars of the frosty night. The high snowdrifts formed humps of snowy hillocks across the narrow track. The top of the covered sledge often knocked against the overhanging branches of the silver firs, shook the hoarfrost from them, trailing noisily under them and dragging them after it. The white surface of the snowy waste reflected the twinkling starlight and lighted up the road. Inside, in the depths of the dense forest, the glittering pall of

snow sent a cold shiver through me; it was just as
though a lighted candle had been stuck in the snow.

Three horses, harnessed in single file, drew the
sledge at a spanking pace, but from time to time one
or the other strayed from the road and left the file.
The coachman drew them back into line again and
again, and when the sledge leaned over to one side he
jumped off it, ran alongside, and supported it with his
shoulder to prevent it from overturning.

I fell asleep again, totally oblivious of the passage of
time, and suddenly woke up from a jolt and the ces-
sation of movement.

The coachmen's inn in the forest was just like one in
a fairy tale about brigands. A dim light in the cottage,
the hissing of the samovar and the ticking of the clock,
the coachman who had just arrived with the sledge is
divesting himself of his coat, thawing himself out, and
talking softly, as one does at night, so as not to wake
the sleepers behind the partition, to the innkeeper's
wife who is about to serve him supper; meanwhile,
another coachman wipes his mustache, buttons up his
peasant overcoat, and goes out into the frost to harness
a team of three horses to another sledge.

And once more a drive at a spanking pace, the
hissing of the runners, dozing, sleep. And then, next
day—a far horizon with factory chimneys, the limit-
less snowy desert of a large frozen river, and a railway.

6

Bobrov treated me with quite undeserved cordiality. He watched unwearyingly over my futuristic purity and protected me from harmful influences. By these he meant the sympathy shown by older people. The moment he noticed any signs of interest on their part, he hastened, fearful lest their kindness should cause me to lapse into academicism, to destroy the suspected bonds of friendship by any means at his disposal. Thanks to him, I never ceased quarrelling with everybody.

I was very fond of Julian Anissimov and his wife, Vera Stanevich. I had to be an involuntary participant of Bobrov's rupture with them.

Vyacheslav Ivanov presented me with one of his books with a moving inscription. In Bryusov's circle of friends, Bobrov made fun of this inscription in a way that suggested that it was I who was responsible for his sneering remarks. Vyacheslav Ivanov stopped speaking to me.

The *Contemporary Review* published my translation of Kleist's comedy *The Broken Jug*. The work was both immature and uninteresting. I should have been deeply grateful to the journal for publishing it. And I ought to have been even more grateful to its editorial board for letting some unknown hand go over my manuscript and improve it beyond recognition.

But the feeling of fairness, modesty, and gratitude

was not fashionable among the young people of the left-wing artistic movements and was looked upon as a sign of sentimentality and spinelessness. The proper thing was to have a high opinion of oneself and one's talents, to strut about, to be impudent, and, however much I hated it, I strove to keep in step with them all so as not to fall behind my friends.

Something had happened to the proofs of the comedy. They were late and they included all sorts of words added by the typesetters which had no relation to the text.

To be fair to Bobrov, it must be stated that in the present case he had no idea what it was all about, and really did not know what he was doing. He said that I should not let such a disgraceful thing as scribbled remarks in the proofs and unasked-for stylistic improvements of the original pass without protest and that I must complain to Gorky, who, according to his information, was in some secret, unofficial way connected with the running of the periodical. I did so. Instead of expressing my thanks to the editorial board of the *Contemporary,* I wrote a stupid letter, full of studied and ignorant arrogance, complaining to Gorky because they had been anxious to help me and had done me a kindness. Years passed and it seems that I complained to Gorky about Gorky. The comedy was published at his recommendation and he corrected it with his own hand.

Finally, my acquaintance with Mayakovsky began

with a polemical meeting of two hostile futuristic groups, he being a member of one of them and I of the other. According to the idea of the organizers of the meeting, it should have ended in a brawl, but a quarrel was averted by the mutual understanding we showed to one another from the very first words.

7

I will not describe my relations with Mayakovsky. We were never on intimate terms. His recognition of myself has been exaggerated. His point of view with regard to my works has been distorted. He disliked my *Year 1905* and *Lieutenant Schmidt* and considered them a mistake. He liked two of my books: *Above the Barriers* and *My Sister, Life*.

I will not describe our meetings and our disagreements. I shall try, as well as I am able, to give a general characterization of Mayakovsky and his significance. Needless to say, both the one and the other will be colored by subjectivity and prejudice.

8

Let us begin with the most important. We have no idea of the mental agony that precedes suicide. Under physical torture on the rack, people lose consciousness every minute, the sufferings inflicted by torture being so great that they bring the end near by the very fact of being so unendurable. Subjected to torture by a hangman, a man is not yet utterly destroyed; though unconscious from pain, he is nevertheless present at his own end, his past belongs to him, his memories are with him, and, if he so desires, he can make use of them and they may be of some help to him before he dies.

Having arrived at the thought of suicide, one abandons all hope, one turns away from one's past, one declares oneself a bankrupt and one's memories as non-existent. These memories are no longer capable of reaching the would-be suicide to save him, to sustain him. The continuity of one's inner existence is destroyed, the personality has ceased to exist. In the end, perhaps, one kills oneself not out of loyalty to the decision one has made, but because one can no longer endure the agony that does not seem to belong to anyone in particular, the suffering in the absence of a sufferer, the empty suspense which is not filled up by a life that still goes on.

It seems to me that Mayakovsky shot himself out of pride because he had condemned something in himself or around himself with which his self-respect could not be reconciled. Esenin hanged himself without any clear realization of the consequences, wondering at heart whether or not it was the end; for you never can tell, it might not be the end after all. Marina Tsvetayeva all her life shielded herself by her work against the humdrum affairs of everyday existence.

When it seemed to her that it was an inadmissible luxury and that for the sake of her son she must for a time sacrifice her all-absorbing passion, she cast a sober look around her and she saw the chaos that had not filtered through her creative work, immovable, stagnant, monstrous, and recoiled in panic. Not knowing how to protect herself from that horror, she hurriedly hid herself in death, putting her head into a noose as under a pillow. I can't help feeling that Paolo Yashvili was no longer capable of comprehending anything at all when, bewitched by the ideas first enunciated by Shigalyov [in Dostoevsky's *The Devils*], which were so prevalent in 1937, he gazed at his sleeping daughter at night and imagined that he was no longer worthy of looking at her and in the morning went to his comrades and blew out his brains with the shot from his double-barrelled gun. And it seems to me that Fadeyev, with that guilty smile which he managed to preserve through all the cunning intricacies of politics, could bid farewell to himself at the last moment before pulling the trigger with, I should imagine, words like these: "Well, it's all over! Good-bye, Sasha!"

But all of them suffered beyond description, their suffering reaching the point where the feeling of anguish became a mental illness. Let us bow our heads with compassion for their talents and their bright memory as well as for their sufferings.

9

And so there was to be a clash between two literary groups in the summer of 1914 in a coffeeshop in the Arbat. Bobrov and I represented one group and Tretyakov and Shershenevich were to represent the other group. But they brought Mayakovsky with them.

It seemed that, contrary to expectation, I was familiar with the appearance of the young man whom I had seen in the corridors of the Fifth Grammar School, where he was two classes below me, and in lobbies of concert halls where I had caught sight of him during the intermissions.

A little earlier one of his future blind admirers had shown me some of Mayakovsky's first published work. In those days that man not only did not understand his future god, but showed me this printed novelty with a scornful laugh as an unmistakably nonsensical piece by a third-rater. But I liked the poems very much. They were his first brightest experiments, which were afterwards published in his collection of poems, *Simple as Mooing*.

Now in the coffeehouse I liked their author no less. Before me sat a handsome youth of gloomy aspect with the bass voice of a deacon and the fist of a pugilist, inexhaustibly, deadly witty, something between a mythical hero of Alexander Grin and a Spanish toreador.

One could see at once that if he was handsome, witty, talented, perhaps supertalented, that was not the main thing about him; the main thing was his innate iron self-control, a kind of inherited principle of nobility, a feeling of duty which did not permit him to be different, less handsome, less witty, less talented.

And this resoluteness of his and his tousled mane of hair, which he kept ruffling with all his five fingers, at once made me think of the young terrorist conspirator, a composite image of the minor provincial characters in Dostoevsky's novels.

The provinces did not always lag behind the Russian capital cities to their own disadvantage. At times, during the period of decadence of the main centers of population, the remote parts of the country were saved by the beneficent old traditions that were preserved there. So, during the reign of the tango and the skating rinks, Mayakovsky brought from the remote Transcaucasian forest district where he was born the conviction, which was still firmly held in out-of-the-way places, that education in Russia could only be revolutionary.

To his natural attributes the young Mayakovsky added, in quite a wonderful fashion, an artistic disorder which he affected and a rather coarse and careless ponderousness of mind and body, and rebellious features of Bohemianism in which he draped himself and with which he played about so tastefully. His taste was so mature and fully developed that it seemed older than himself. He was twenty-two, and his taste was, as it were, a hundred and twenty-two.

10

I liked Mayakovsky's early lyrical poetry very much. Against the background of buffoonery that was so characteristic of those days, its seriousness—so heavy, so menacing, and so plaintive—was quite unusual. It was a poetry beautifully modelled, majestic, demonic, and, at the same time, infinitely doomed, perishing and almost calling for help.

> *Time, I beseech you: though you be*
> *A blind ikon painter, my image paint*
> *In the shrine of this century's abortion!*
> *I am solitary like the one-eyed*
> *Man who goes to lead the blind.*

Time obliged and did what he asked. His image is written in the shrine of our century. But what one had to possess to see and divine it!
Or he says:

> *Not for you to understand why, calm*
> *Amid the storm of gibes,*
> *My soul I carry on a plate*
> *For the feast of coming years. . . .*

It is impossible not to think of parallels from the liturgy: "Be silent, all flesh of man, and stand in fear

93

and trembling and think not of earthly things. For the King of Kings and the Lord of Lords cometh to offer Himself as a sacrifice and as food to the faithful."

In contradiction to the classics, to whom the sense of the hymns and prayers was important, to Pushkin, who paraphrased St. Yefrem of Syria in his *Desert Fathers,* and to Alexey Tolstoy, who put into verse the funeral lamentations of St. John of Damascus, the fragments of Church canticles and lessons are dear to Blok, Mayakovsky, and Esenin in their literal sense, as fragments of everyday life, in the same way as the street, the house, and any words of colloquial speech are dear to them.

These ancient literary deposits suggested to Mayakovsky the parodical structure of his poems. One can find in him a great many analogies with canonical ideas, hidden or underlined. They called for something vast and mighty, they demanded strong hands and trained the poet's audacity.

It is a very good thing that Mayakovsky and Esenin did not ignore what they knew and remembered from childhood, that they raised these familiar strata, made use of the beauty contained in them and did not leave them under lock and key.

II

When I got to know Mayakovsky more intimately, we discovered that there were unforeseen, technical

Vladimir Mayakovsky, by G. Annenkov

coincidences in our poems, a similar construction of images, a similarity of rhyme structure. I liked the beauty and the felicity of his movements. I did not want anything better. Not to repeat him and not to seem to be his imitator, I began to suppress in myself everything I had in common with him, the heroic tone, which would have been false in my case, and the desire for effects. This narrowed down my style and purified it.

Mayakovsky had neighbors. He was not a solitary figure in poetry, he was not in a desert. Before the Revolution his rival on the concert platform was Igor Severyanin and, in the arena of the people's revolution and in the hearts of men—Sergey Esenin.

Severyanin was the dictator of the concert halls and when he appeared the house, to use a theatrical term, was sold out. He used to sing his verses to two or three popular tunes from French operas, without its becoming vulgar or offending the ear.

His lack of culture, his bad taste and vulgar coinage of words in combination with the pure and unimpeded flow of his poetic diction created a special strange genre representing, under the cloak of banality, a belated appearance of Turgenev's influence in poetry.

Since the days of Koltsov, Russia has not produced anything so native, natural, appropriate, and inalienable as Sergey Esenin, having made him a present to our times with unexampled freedom and without burdening her present with tons of ultranationalistic zeal.

At the same time, Esenin was a living, palpitating particle of that spirit of pure art which, after Pushkin, we call the highest Mozartean principle, the Mozartean element.

Esenin treated his life like a fairy tale. He was Ivan the Crown Prince who flew over the ocean on a gray wolf and, like the Firebird, caught Isadora Duncan by the tail. His verses, too, he wrote by fairy tale methods, sometimes arranging his words like cards in a game of patience and sometimes writing them with his heart's blood. The most precious thing in him is the image of his native countryside, the woodlands of central Russia, of the Ryazan province, described with amazing freshness as it appeared to him in childhood.

Compared with Esenin, Mayakovsky's genius was coarser and more ponderous but, to make up for it, perhaps vaster and more profound. The place nature occupies in Esenin is occupied in Mayakovsky's poetry by the labyrinth of a modern big city, where the solitary soul of modern man has lost its way and become morally entangled and whose passionate and inhuman situations he depicts.

12

As I have said already, my intimacy with Mayakovsky has been exaggerated. Once, at Aseyev's, where we had a discussion about our differences, which have become more acute since then, he characterized our dissimilarity in these words: "Well, what does it matter? We really are different. You love lightning in the sky and I in an electric iron!"

I could not understand his propagandist zeal, the worming of himself and his friends by force into the public's consciousness, his idea that a poem could be written by several hands, by an association of craftsmen, and his complete subordination to the demand for topical subjects.

Even more incomprehensible to me was the journal *Lef* which he edited, its contributors and the system of ideas which was defended in it. The only consistent and honest man in this group of negationists was Sergey Tretyakov, who drove his negation to its natural conclusion. Like Plato, Tretyakov considered that there was no place for art in a young socialist state, or, at any rate, not at the moment of its birth, and that the commonplace pseudo-art, uncreative and vitiated by the corrections made in accordance with the dictates of the times, which flourished in *Lef,* was not worth the worries and labors lavished on it, and that it could be easily sacrificed.

With the exception of the immortal document *At the Top of the Voice,* written on the eve of his death, the later Mayakovsky, beginning with *Mystery Buffo,* is inaccessible to me. I remain indifferent to those clumsily rhymed sermons, that cultivated insipidity, those commonplaces and platitudes, set forth so artificially, so confusedly, and so devoid of humor. This

Mayakovsky is in my view worthless, that is, non-existent. And the remarkable thing about it is that this worthless, nonexistent Mayakovsky has come to be accepted as revolutionary.

But it was a general mistake to consider that Mayakovsky and I were friends. Thus, for instance, Esenin, at the period of his dissatisfaction with imagism, asked me to arrange a meeting with Mayakovsky because he was anxious to become reconciled with him and because he thought that I was the right man for the job.

Though I was on familiar terms with Esenin, and not with Mayakovsky, my meetings with the former were even more infrequent. They could be counted on the fingers of the hands and they always ended in stormy scenes. We either shed tears and vowed to be true to one another, or engaged in violent fights and had to be separated by force.

13

During the last years of Mayakovsky's life, when all poetry had ceased to exist, either his or anybody else's, when Esenin had hanged himself, when, to put it more simply, literature had stopped—for even the beginning of *Quiet Flows the Don* and the first works of Pilnyak and Babel, Fedin and Vsevolod Ivanov, were poetry—in those years Mayakovsky's closest friend and his principal supporter was Aseyev, a perfect comrade, intelligent, talented, inwardly free, and unblinded by anything.

I, on the other hand, had completely broken with him, but for some reason, in spite of my announcement about my resignation from *Lef* and my ceasing to be a member of their circle, my name continued to appear among the names of contributors. I wrote a sharply worded letter to Mayakovsky which should have made him boil with rage.

A little earlier, during the years when I was still under the spell of his fire, his inner force, and his immense creative powers, and when he returned my devotion with the same warmth, I inscribed eight lines of verse in his copy of my *My Sister, Life*. In these I deplored his preoccupation with the national balance sheet and the tragedy of the Supreme Council of National Economy, and expressed my surprise that he should have strayed from his true and sincere path and allowed himself to be inveigled "under the arches of such an almshouse."

14

There are two famous sayings about that period: that life had become easier and more cheerful; and that Mayakovsky was and remained the best and most talented poet of the epoch. For the second saying I thanked the author in a personal letter, for it pro-

tected me from the inflation of my role, to which I
had become assigned in the mid-thirties, at the time of
the Writers' Conference. I like my life and I am
satisfied with it. I am not in need of any additional
gilding of it. Life without privacy and without ob-
scurity, life reflected in the splendor of a plate-glass
show case is inconceivable to me.

Mayakovsky was beginning to be propagated com-
pulsorily, like potatoes in the reign of Catherine the
Great. That was his second death. For that he is not to
blame.

Alexander Scriabin,
by L. Pasternak

Alexander Blok

THREE SHADOWS

THREE SEASIDE

In July, 1917, Ehrenburg got in touch with me on the advice of Bryusov. It was then that I got to know this clever writer, active and unreserved and with a cast of mind so different from mine.

It was then that the great influx began of political *émigrés* returning from abroad, people who had been caught abroad by the war and interned, and many others. Andrey Bely arrived from Switzerland. Ehrenburg arrived.

Ehrenburg spoke to me in high terms of Marina Tsvetayeva and showed me her poems. I was present at a literary meeting at the beginning of the Revolution at which she, among other writers, read her verses. During one of the winters of the Civil War I went to see her with some kind of message. I talked about all sorts of unimportant things and listened to all sorts of trivialities in turn. Marina Tsvetayeva made no impression on me.

My ear was at the time perverted by the pretentious extravagances and the break from everything natural that were in vogue in those days. Everything spoken in a normal way rebounded from me. I forgot that words by themselves can mean and contain something apart from the cheap toys with which they are strung.

It was just the harmony of Marina Tsvetayeva's

verses, the clarity of their meaning, the presence of fine qualities and absence of defects that interfered with and barred the way to my understanding of their true nature. It was not the essential I looked for in everything, but some nicety which had nothing to do with it.

For a long time I underestimated Marina Tsvetayeva as in different ways I had underestimated Bagritsky, Khlebnikov, Mandelstam, and Gumilyov.

I have already said that among the young people who could not express themselves intelligibly and who raised their tongue-tied babblings into a virtue and tried to be original at all costs, only two, Aseyev and Marina Tsvetayeva, expressed themselves in human language and wrote in a classical style and language.

And suddenly both of them renounced their skill. Aseyev was tempted by Khlebnikov's example. Marina Tsvetayeva had undergone some inward changes of her own. But it was the original, the traditional Marina Tsvetayeva who in the end prevailed over me long before she suffered a rebirth.

2

One had to read oneself into her. When I had done so, I was amazed to discover such an abyss of purity and power. Nothing at all comparable existed anywhere else. Let me be brief. I don't think I shall go far wrong if I say that with the exception of Annensky and Blok and, with certain reservations, Andrey Bely, the early Marina Tsvetayeva was what all the rest of the symbolists taken together wanted to be but were not. Where their literary efforts floundered helplessly in a world of artificial contrivances and lifeless archaisms, Marina Tsvetayeva skimmed with the greatest of ease over the difficulties of true creative art, solving its problems with remarkable facility and with incomparable technical brilliance.

In the spring of 1922, when she was already abroad, I bought in Moscow her little volume *Versts*. I was instantly won over by the great lyrical power of the form of her poetry, which stemmed from personal experience, which was not weak-chested but wonderfully compact and condensed, which did not get out of breath at the end of each separate line, but which by the development of its periods without interruption of rhythm sustained itself for a whole succession of strophes.

These peculiarities seemed to conceal a sort of closeness or, perhaps, a community of experienced influences, or a similarity of stimuli in the formation of character, a resemblance in the part played by family and music, a homogeneity of points of departure, aims, and preferences.

I wrote a letter to Marina Tsvetayeva in Prague full of expressions of my enthusiasm and my surprise that

I had failed to recognize her genius for so long and had made myself familiar with her work so late. She replied to my letter. We began a correspondence which grew particularly frequent in the middle of the twenties after the appearance of her *Craftsmanship*. In Moscow her other poems became known in manuscript, poems that were outstanding for the sweep of their ideas and brilliant and quite extraordinary for their novelty, such as *The Poem of the End, The Poem of the Mountain,* and *The Ratcatcher*. We became friends.

In the summer of 1935, feeling ill and on the point of a breakdown from insomnia lasting for almost a year, I found myself at an anti-Fascist congress in Paris. There I became acquainted with Marina Tsvetayeva's husband, a charming, refined, and steadfast man, and I grew fond of him as if he were my own brother.

The members of Marina Tsvetayeva's family insisted that she should return to Russia. They were prompted partly by homesickness and sympathy with Communism and the Soviet Union and partly by the consideration that Marina Tsvetayeva could never be happy in Paris and that she would perish living in a sort of vacuum without any readers to respond to her.

Marina Tsvetayeva asked me what I thought of it. I had no definite opinion to offer. I did not know what to say to her and I was very much afraid that she and her remarkable family would find things rather dif-

ficult and not very peaceful in Russia. The general
tragedy of the family infinitely exceeded my fears.

3

At the beginning of this autobiographical sketch, in
the section referring to my childhood, I gave some de-
scriptions of real scenes and pictures and related a
number of true events, and in the middle I went over
to generalizations and began to limit my story to rapid
characterizations. I am afraid this had to be done for
the sake of compactness.

Had I begun to relate the story of my friendship with
Marina Tsvetayeva incident by incident, the history of
the aspirations and interests that created the common
bond between her and myself, I should have digressed
too far from the limits which I had imposed upon
myself. I should have had to devote a whole book
to it, so many things had we experienced in common,
changes, joyful and tragic events, always unexpected,
and time after time enlarging the mental outlook of
us both.

But here, too, and in the remaining chapters, I shall
refrain from anything personal and limit myself to
what is essential and of general interest.

Marina Tsvetayeva was a woman with the soul of
an active man, determined, militant, indomitable. In
her life and in her work she rushed impetuously,
eagerly, and almost rapaciously toward the achieve-

ment of finality and definitiveness, in the pursuit of which she had gone far and was ahead of everybody else.

In addition to the small number of her known poems, she wrote a great number of things that are not generally known, immense, violent works, some in the style of Russian fairy tales, others on subjects of well-known historical legends and myths.

Their publication would be a great triumph and a great find for Russian poetry. It would be a belated gift that would enrich it all at once.

I think that a thorough re-examination of her work and the fullest possible recognition of her genius await Marina Tsvetayeva.

We were friends. I had about a hundred letters from her in reply to mine. In spite of the place that losses and disappearances, as I have explained earlier, occupied in my life, I could never have visualized the loss of these carefully kept precious letters. They were lost because of overcarefulness in guarding them.

During the war years and my visits to my evacuated family, one of the members of the staff of the Scriabin Museum, a great admirer of Marina Tsvetayeva and a great friend of mine, proposed to me that I should give her these letters, together with the letters of my parents and several letters from Gorky and Romain Rolland, for safekeeping. She put them in the Museum safe, but kept Marina Tsvetayeva's letters with her, not wishing to let them out of her hands and distrusting the strength of the walls of the fireproof safe.

She lived all the year round outside Moscow and every evening she carried the letters home with her in an attaché case and took them back to the museum in the morning. One winter night she was going back to her house in the country in a state of utter exhaustion. Halfway from the station, in the woods, she suddenly realized that she had left the attaché case with the letters in the train. That is how Marina Tsvetayeva's letters went astray and got lost.

4

During the decades since the publication of *Safe Conduct,* I often thought that if I were to republish it I would add a chapter on the Caucasus and two Georgian poets. Time passed and the need for other additions did not arise. The only gap that remained was this missing chapter. I am going to write it now.

About 1930, in winter, Paolo Yashvili and his wife paid me a visit in Moscow. Yashvili was a brilliant man of the world, a cultured and entertaining conversationalist, a "European," a tall and handsome man.

Soon after their visit all sorts of upheavals, complications, and changes took place in two families, that of a friend of mine and my own. They were very painful to those implicated in them. For some time my companion, who was afterwards to become my second wife, and I had no roof over our heads. Yashvili offered us a place of refuge at his house in Tiflis.

At that time the Caucasus, Georgia, the life of the Georgian people and some of its individual representatives were a complete revelation to me. Everything was new, everything was surprising. Dark bulks of overhanging mountains towered at the end of all the street vistas of Tiflis. The life of the city's poorest inhabitants, brought out from the yards into the streets, was bolder and less concealed than in the North. It was brighter and more candid. It was full of mysticism and the messianic symbolism of folk legends which are so favorable to the life of the imagination and which, as in Catholic Poland, turn every man into a poet. The more advanced section of the population showed a high level of cultural and intellectual life that was seldom to be met with in those days. The fine buildings of certain parts of Tiflis reminded me of Petersburg; some had railings outside the first-floor windows which were bent in the shape of baskets or lyres. The city also abounded in picturesque back lanes. Big tambourines beating to the rhythm of the *lezginka* followed you about everywhere and always seemed to catch up with you. In addition, there were the goat-like bleatings of the bagpipes and some other musical instruments. Nightfall in a Southern town was full of stars and the scent of flowers from the gardens mingled with the smells from coffeehouses and confectioners' shops.

Paolo Yashvili is a remarkable poet of the post-

словно в узелках от мелькания больших и малых снежинок.
Мужчины входили с холода в болтающихся на ногах глубо-
ких ботиках и поголовно корчили из себя рассеянных и не-
уклюжих увальней, а их посвежевшие на морозе жены в рас-
стегнутых на две верхних пуговицы шубках и сбившихся
назад пуховых платках на заиндевевших волосах, наоборот,
изображали прожженных ведьм, само коварство, пальца в
рот не клади. "Племянник Кюи" - пронесся шопот, когда
приехал новый, в первый раз в этот дом приглашенный пианист.

Из зала через растворенные в двух концах боковые
двери виднелся длинный, как зимняя дорога, накрытый стол
в столовой. В глаза бросалась яркая игра рябиновки в бу-
Воображение пленяли
тылках с зернистой гранью, *и судки с маслом и уксусом в*
маленьких графинчиках на серебряных подставках, *живопис-*
и Само сложенные пирамидами салфетки, стойкою и заmanu-
ность дичи и закусок, ~~стоял на~~
~~~~ *ковых которых прибор, и пахнувшие миндалем синели-*
ягоды цикория в корзинах, казалось, дразнили аппетит.
~~~~ чтобы не
нн
отдалять желанного мига вкушения земной пищи, поторопи-
лись как можно скорее обратиться к духовной. Расселись
в зале рядами. "Племянник Кюи", - возобновился шопот,
когда пианист занял свое место за инструментом. Концерт
начался.

Про сонату знали, что она скучная и замученная, го-
ловная. Она оправдала ожидания, да к тому же еще оказа-
лась страшно растянутой.

Об этом в перерыве спорили критик Керимбеков с
Александром Александровичем. Критик ругал сонату, а Але-

Doctor Zhivago—ms. page with corrections by Pasternak

symbolist period. His poetry is constructed on exact data and the evidence of the senses. It is akin to the modern European prose of Bely, Hamsun, and Proust and, like that prose, is fresh with unexpected and accurate observations. It is creative poetry *par excellence*. It is not cluttered up with tightly crammed effects. It is spacious and airy. It moves and breathes.

5

The First World War caught Yashvili in Paris. He was a student at the Sorbonne. He returned to his native country by a roundabout route. At a remote Norwegian railway station, Yashvili, lost in a daydream, did not notice that his train had left. A young Norwegian married couple, a farmer and his wife, who had come by sledge from their remote village for the post, saw the daydreaming, fiery Southerner and the unfortunate result of his daydreams. They were sorry for Yashvili and, after succeeding somehow or other in making themselves understood, took him with them to their farm where he was to stay till the next train which was only expected in two days' time.

Yashvili was a marvellous raconteur. He was a born teller of adventure stories. He was always beset by the sort of surprises that one only reads about in novels. Chance played a prominent part in his life. He had a gift for it. He was lucky that way.

In his company one could not help feeling that one was in the presence of a highly gifted man. His eyes blazed with the fire of his soul, his lips were seared by the fire of his passions. His face was scorched and blackened by the heat of experience, so that he seemed to be older than his age, a man who had been through a great deal, a man who was a little the worse for wear.

On the day of our arrival he collected his friends, the members of the group whose leader he was. I don't remember who came on that occasion. His next-door neighbor, Nikolay Nadiradze, must quite certainly have been there. Titian Tabidze was there too with his wife.

6

I can see that room just as if I were there now. And how could I forget it? On that very evening, without suspecting the horrors that lay in store for it, I lowered it very gently so that it should not get broken to the bottom of my soul with all the terrible things that happened in it and near it.

Why were those two men sent to me? How shall I describe our relations? Both became integral parts of my personal world. I did not prefer one to the other because they were inseparable and complementary to one another. The fate of these two men, and that of Marina Tsvetayeva, was to become my greatest sorrow.

7

If Yashvili was turned outwards, all in a centrifugal direction, Titian Tabidze was turned inwards and every line he wrote and every step he took called you into the depths of his rich soul, so full of intuitions and forebodings.

The main thing in his poetry is the feeling of an inexhaustible fund of lyrical potentialities that is implied in every one of his poems, the preponderance of unsaid things and of those he would still say over those he had said already. This presence of an untouched store of spiritual reserves creates the background and lends depth to his poems and imparts that special mood with which they are imbued and which constitutes their principal and bitter charm. There is as much soul in his poems as there was in himself, a complex, esoteric soul, directed wholly toward good, capable of clairvoyance and self-sacrifice.

When I think of Yashvili all sorts of urban scenes come to my mind, rooms, arguments, addresses delivered at public meetings, Yashvili's dazzling eloquence at crowded parties at night.

The thought of Tabidze brings to mind the elements of nature, in my imagination arise all sorts of country scenes, the freedom of flowering meadows, the waves of the sea.

Clouds are sailing along, and in the distance, in a

line with them, mountains rise up. And the thickset, compact figure of the smiling poet merges with them. He has a somewhat wavering gait. He shakes all over when he laughs. Now he gets up, stands sideways to the table, and taps his glass with a knife before making a speech. His habit of raising one shoulder higher than the other makes him look a little crooked.

His house in Kodzhary stands at the bend of the road. The road rises along the front and then, bending round the house, goes past its back wall. From that house one can see those who walk and those who drive past it twice.

It was at the height of the period when, according to Bely's witty definition, the triumph of materialism had abolished matter. There was nothing to eat; there was nothing to wear. There was nothing tangible around, only ideas. If we kept alive, it was thanks to our Tiflis friends, miracle workers who all the time managed to get something and bring something and provide us with advances from publishing houses for something we had no idea of.

We met, exchanged news, dined, read something to each other. The light, cool breezes played, as though with fingers, with the poplar's silvery foliage, velvety and white on the underside. The air, as with rumors, was full of the heavy scents of the South. Like the front of a cart on its coupling-pole, the night on high slowly turned the whole body of its starry chariot. And on the road bullock-carts and automobiles drove and moved along and every one of them could be seen from the house twice.

Or we were on the Georgian military road, or in Borzhom, or in Abastuman. Or after trips into the countryside, to beauty spots, adventures, and libations, we, each one of us with something or other, and I with a black eye from a fall, stopped in Bakuriany at the house of Leonidze, a most original poet, more than anyone else closely bound up with the mysteries of the language in which he wrote, and for that reason least of all amenable to translation.

A midnight feast on the grass in a wood, a beautiful hostess, two charming little daughters. Next day the unexpected arrival of a *mestvir,* a wandering minstrel with a bagpipe, and an impromptu glorification of everyone at the table in turn, with an appropriate text and an ability to seize on any excuse, like my black eye, for instance, for a toast.

Or we went to the seaside in Kabuleti. Rains and storms. In the same hotel Simon Chikovani, the future master of bright, picturesque verse, at the time still a member of the Communist Youth League. And above the line of all the mountains and horizons, the head of the smiling poet walking beside me, and the bright, luminous signs of his prodigious talent, and the shadow of sadness and destiny in his smile. And once more I bid farewell to him now on these pages. Let me, in his person, bid a farewell to all my other memories.

CONCLUSION
—

This concludes my autobiographical sketch. I do not cut it short by leaving it unfinished, but put a full stop where I had intended to put it from the very first. It was not my intention to write the history of the last fifty years in many volumes and with many characters.

I have not analyzed the works of Martynov, Zabolotsky, Selvinsky, Tikhonov—all good poets. I have not said anything about the poets of the generation of Simonov and Tvardovsky, so numerous.

I proceeded from the center of the narrowest circle of life, limiting myself by it deliberately.

What I have written here is enough to give an idea of how life in my own case was transmuted into art, how it was born of chance and experience. . . .

Above I have described my ambivalent attitude toward my own poetic past and to that of others. I would never lift a finger to bring back from oblivion three fourths of what I have written. Why then, it may be objected, do I let someone else publish it?

There are two reasons for it. First, there are often grains of truth, aptness, and acute observation in the mass of what is deplorable and annoying about those things of mine. Secondly, quite recently, I completed my chief and most important work, the only one I am not ashamed of and for which I can answer with the utmost confidence, a novel in prose with a supplement in verse, *Doctor Zhivago*.

I have now come to the end of my autobiographical sketch. To continue it would be exceedingly difficult. To keep up the sequence of events I should have had to speak of years, circumstances, people, and destinies within the framework of the Revolution. Of a world of hitherto unknown aims and aspirations, problems and exploits, a new self-restraint, a new strictness—new trials with which this world confronts the human personality and man's honor, pride, and endurance.

This unique world, the like of which has never been known before, has now receded into the faraway distance of memories and hangs suspended on the horizon like mountains seen from a plain or like a faraway big city against the smoky background of a red sunset.

One would have to write about it in a way to make the heart stop beating and the hair stand on end. To write about it in an ordinary and commonplace way, to write about it unemotionally, to write about it less colorfully than Gogol and Dostoevsky have depicted Petersburg, is not only senseless and useless; to write like that would be both dishonest and base.

We are far from that ideal.

November, 1957

TRANSLATING
SHAKESPEARE

—

Published in *Literary Moscow*, Almanac of the Moscow Writers, edited by
M. I. Aliger and others, 1956. Only two issues of the almanac appeared;
Pasternak's article was published in the first issue.
This translation is by MANYA HARARI.

Over the years I have translated several of Shakespeare's plays: *Hamlet, Romeo and Juliet, Antony and Cleopatra, Othello, King Henry IV* (Parts I and II), *King Lear* and *Macbeth*.

The demand for simple and readable translations is great and seemingly inexhaustible. Every translator flatters himself with the hope that he, more than others, will succeed in meeting it. I have not escaped the common fate.

Nor are my opinions on the aims and problems of translating literary works exceptional. I believe, as do many others, that closeness to the original is not ensured only by literal exactness or by similarity of form: the likeness, as in a portrait, cannot be achieved without a lively and natural method of expression. As much as the author, the translator must confine himself to a vocabulary which is natural to him and avoid the literary artifice involved in stylization. Like the original text, the translation must create an impression of life and not of verbiage.

Shakespeare's Poetic Style

Shakespeare's dramas are deeply realistic in their conception. In his prose passages and in those dialogues in verse which are combined with movement or action his style is conversational. For the rest, the flow of his blank verse is highly metaphorical, sometimes needlessly so and in such cases at the cost of some artificiality.

His imagery is not always equal to itself. At times it is poetry at its highest, at others it falls plainly into rhetoric and is loaded with dozens of inadequate substitutes for the one right word which he had on the tip of his tongue and which escaped him in his hurry. Nevertheless, at its worst as at its best, his metaphorical speech conforms to the essentials of true allegory.

Metaphorical language is the result of the disproportion between man's short life and the immense and long-term tasks he sets himself. Because of this, he needs to look at things as sharply as an eagle and to convey his vision in flashes which can be immediately apprehended. This is just what poetry is. Outsize personalities use metaphor as a shorthand of the spirit.

The stormy quickness of the brushstrokes of a Rembrandt, a Michelangelo, or a Titian was not the fruit of their deliberate choice. Possessed by the need to paint the universe, they could not paint in any other way.

Shakespeare's style combines opposite extremes. His prose is finished and polished. It is the work of a genius in the art of comic detail, a master of conciseness, and a brilliant mimic of everything strange and curious in the world.

In complete contrast to this is his blank verse. Vol-

I take the opportunity to repeat you, that except the "Dr. Zh." which you should read, all the rest of my very and writings are devoid of any sense and importance.

The most part of my native year I gave off to Goethe, Shakespeare and other great and voluminary Translators.

Thankfully your

B. P.

Facsimile of a letter written in October, 1958

taire and Tolstoy were shocked by its inward and outward chaos.

Shakespeare's characters, who often go through several stages of completion, occasionally speak first in poetry and later in prose. In such cases the scenes in verse produce the impression of being sketches and those in prose of being finished and conclusive.

Verse was Shakespeare's most rapid and immediate method of expression. It was his quickest way of putting down his thoughts. So true is this that many of his verse passages read almost like the rough drafts of his prose.

His poetry draws its strength from its very quality of sketchiness, powerful, uncontrollable, disorderly, and abundant.

Shakespeare's Use of Rhythm

Shakespeare's rhythm is the basic principle of his poetry. Its momentum determines the speed and sequence of questions and answers in his dialogues and the length of his periods and monologues.

It is a rhythm which reflects the enviably laconic quality of English, a quality which makes it possible to compress a whole statement, made up of two or more contrasted propositions, into a single line of iambic verse. It is the rhythm of free speech, the language of a man who sets up no idols and is therefore honest and concise.

Hamlet

Shakespeare's use of rhythm is clearest in *Hamlet,* where it serves a triple purpose. It is used as a method of characterization, it makes audible and sustains the prevailing mood, and it elevates the tone and softens the brutality of certain scenes.

The characters are sharply differentiated by the rhythm of their speech. Polonius, the King, Guildenstern and Rosencrantz speak in one way, Laertes, Ophelia, Horatio, and the rest in another. The credulity of the Queen is shown not only in her words but also by her singsong manner of drawing out her vowels.

So vivid is the rhythmic characterization of Hamlet himself that it creates the illusion of a leitmotif, as though a musical phrase were reiterated at his every appearance on the stage, although in fact no such leitmotif exists. The very pulse of his being seems to be made audible. Everything is contained in it: his inconsistent gestures, his long, resolute stride and the proud half-turn of his head, as well as the way in which the thoughts he utters in his monologues leap and take flight, the mocking arrogance of his ripostes to the courtiers who mill round him, and his manner of staring into the distance of the unknown whence his father's ghost once summoned him and where it may at any moment speak again.

Neither the music of Hamlet's speech nor that of

the play as a whole lends itself to quotation: it is impossible to give an impression of it by any one example. Yet, disembodied though it is, so ominously and so closely is it woven into the texture of the tragedy that, given the subject, one is tempted to describe it as Scandinavian and as suited to the climate of apparitions. It consists in a measured alternation of solemnity and disquiet and, by thickening the atmosphere to its utmost density, it brings out the dominant mood. What is this mood?

According to the well-established view of critics, *Hamlet* is a tragedy of the will. This is true. But in what sense is it to be understood? Absence of will power did not exist as a theme in Shakespeare's time: it aroused no interest. Nor does Shakespeare's portrait of Hamlet, drawn so clearly and in so much detail, suggest a neurotic. Hamlet is a prince of the blood who never, for a moment, ceases to be conscious of his rights as heir to the throne; he is the spoilt darling of an ancient court, and self-assured in the awareness of his natural gifts. The sum of qualities with which he is endowed by Shakespeare leaves no room for flabbiness: it precludes it. Rather, the opposite is true: the audience, impressed by his brilliant prospects, is left to judge of the greatness of his sacrifice in giving them up for a higher aim.

From the moment of the ghost's appearance, Hamlet gives up his will in order to "do the will of him that sent him." *Hamlet* is not a drama of weakness, but of duty and self-denial. It is immaterial that, when appearance and reality are shown to be at variance—to be indeed separated by an abyss—the message is conveyed by supernatural means and that the ghost commands Hamlet to exact vengeance. What is important is that chance has allotted Hamlet the role of judge of his own time and servant of the future. *Hamlet* is the drama of a high destiny, of a life devoted and preordained to a heroic task.

This is the overall tone of the play, so concentrated by the rhythm as to be almost palpable. But the rhythmic principle is applied in still another way. It has a softening effect on certain harsh scenes which would be intolerable without it.

Thus for instance, in the scene in which he sends Ophelia to a nunnery, Hamlet speaks to the girl who loves him, and whom he tramples underfoot, with the ruthlessness of a self-centered Byronic rebel. His irony is out of keeping with his own love for her, which he painfully suppresses in himself. But let us see how this heartless scene is introduced. Immediately before it comes the famous speech, "To be or not to be," and the fresh music of the monologue still echoes in the opening verses which Hamlet and Ophelia exchange. The bitter and disorderly beauty of the monologue in which Hamlet's perplexities crowd and overtake each other and remain unsolved recalls the sudden chords, abruptly cut off, tried out on the organ before the opening of a requiem.

No wonder that the monologue heralds the beginning of the cruel dénouement. It precedes it as the funeral service precedes the burial. The way is opened by it for whatever is inevitable, and whatever follows is washed, redeemed, and lent majesty in advance not only by the spoken thoughts but by the ardor and purity of the tears which ring in it.

Romeo and Juliet

If such is the importance of rhythm in *Hamlet,* we might expect it to be greater still in *Romeo and Juliet.* Where, if not in a drama of first love, should harmony and measure have free play? But Shakespeare puts them to an unexpected use. He shows us that lyricism is not what we imagined it to be. He composes no arias, no duets. His intuition leads him by a different path.

Music plays a negative role in *Romeo and Juliet.* It is on the side of the forces which are hostile to the lovers, the forces of worldly hypocrisy and of the hustle of daily life.

Until he meets Juliet, Romeo is full of his imaginary passion for Rosaline, who never appears on the stage. His romantic pose is in the current fashion of his time. It drives him out on solitary walks at night and he makes up for lost sleep by day, shaded by closed shutters from the sun. All the time that this is going on, in the first scenes of the play, he speaks unnaturally in rhymed verse, melodiously declaiming his high-falutin nonsense in the affected drawing-room manner of his day. But from the moment when he sees Juliet at the ball and stops dead in front of her, not a trace is left of his tuneful mode of expression.

Compared to other feelings, love is an elemental cosmic force wearing a disguise of meekness. In itself it is as simple and unconditional as consciousness and as death, as oxygen or uranium. It is not a state of mind, it is the foundation of the universe. Being thus basic and primordial, it is the equal of artistic creation. Its dignity is no less, and its expression has no need of art to polish it. The most that the artist can dream of is to overhear its voice, to catch its ever new, ever unprecedented language. Love has no need of euphony. Truth, not sound, dwells in its heart.

Like all Shakespeare's plays, *Romeo and Juliet* is written for the most part in blank verse, and it is in blank verse that the hero and heroine address each other. But the measure is never stressed, it is never obvious. There is no declamation. The form never asserts itself at the expense of the infinitely discreet content. This is poetry at its best, and like all such poetry it has the freshness and simplicity of prose. Romeo and Juliet speak in half tones, their conversation is guarded, interrupted, secret. It has the very sound of high emotion and mortal danger overheard at night.

The only noisy and emphatically rhythmic scenes

are those in crowded rooms and streets. Out in the street, where the blood of Montagues and Capulets is shed, ring the daggers of the quarrelling clans. Cooks quarrel and clatter knives in the kitchen as they cook the endless dinners. And to this din of butchery and cooking, as to the brassy beat of a noisy band, the quiet tragedy of feeling develops, spoken for the most part in the soundless whispers of conspirators.

Othello

The division of the plays into acts and scenes was not made by Shakespeare but later, by his editors. Nevertheless it was not forced on them: they lend themselves to it easily by virtue of their inward structure.

The original texts, printed without a break, nevertheless stood out by a rigor of construction and development which is rare in our time.

This applies particularly to the thematic development usually contained in the middle of the drama, that is to say in the third and some parts of the second and fourth acts. This section is, as it were, the box which holds the mainspring of the mechanism.

At the beginning and conclusion of his plays Shakespeare freely improvises the details and, with as light a heart, disposes of the loose ends. The swiftly changing scenes are full of life, they are drawn from nature with the utmost freedom and with a staggering wealth of imagination.

But he denies himself this freedom in the middle section, where the threads have been tied up and must begin to be unravelled; here Shakespeare shows himself to be the child and slave of his age. His third acts are riveted to the mechanics of the plot in a measure unknown to the dramatic art of later centuries, though it was from him that it learned its honesty and daring. They are ruled by too blind a faith in the power of logic and in the real existence of ethical abstractions. The lively portraits drawn at the beginning, with their convincing light and shade, are replaced by personified virtues and vices. The sequence of actions and events ceases to be natural and has the suspect tidiness of rational deductions, as of syllogisms in an argument.

When Shakespeare was a child, moralities constructed in accordance with the formal rules of medieval scholasticism were still shown on the English provincial stage. He may well have seen them, and his old-fashioned industry in working out his plot may have been a remnant of the past which had fascinated him in his childhood.

Four-fifths of his writings are made up of his beginnings and endings. This is the part that made the audience laugh and cry; it is on this that his fame is based, and it accounts for all the talk about his truthfulness to life in opposition to the deadly soullessness of neoclassicism.

But a thing may be rightly observed, yet wrongly explained. One often hears extravagant praise of the "mousetrap" in *Hamlet* or of the iron necessity in the development of this or that passion or in the consequences of this or that crime in Shakespeare. Such admiration starts from false premises. It is not the mousetrap that deserves to be admired, but Shakespeare's genius which shows itself even where his writing is artificial. What should cause wonder is that the third acts, which make up one-fifth of his work and which are often devitalized and contrived, do not circumvent his greatness. He survives, not because of, but in spite of them.

For all the passion and the genius concentrated in *Othello,* and for all its popularity on the stage, what has been said above applies in a considerable measure to this play.

Here we have the dazzling quays of Venice, Brabantio's house, the arsenal; the extraordinary night session of the Senate, and Othello's account of the gradual beginnings of his and Desdemona's feeling for each other. Then the storm at sea off the coast of Cyprus and the drunken brawl at night on the ramparts. And, before the end, the famous scene of Desdemona preparing for the night, in which the still more famous "Willow" song is sung, tragically natural before the dreadful illumination of the finale.

But what happens in between? With a few turns of the key, Iago winds up like an alarm clock the suspicions of his victim, and the course of jealousy, obvious and labored, unwinds, creaking and shuddering like a rusty mechanism. It will be said that such is the nature of jealousy or that such is the tribute paid to the convention of the stage with its insistence on excessive clarity. It may be so. But the damage would be less if the tribute were paid by an artist of less genius and less consistency. In our time another aspect of the play has a topical interest.

Can it be an accident that the hero is black, while all that he holds dear in life is white? What is the significance of this choice of colors? Does it mean only that all peoples have an equal right to human dignity? Shakespeare's thought went much further.

The concept of the equality of peoples did not exist in his time. What did exist and was fully alive was a different and wider notion of their equal opportunities. Shakespeare was not interested in what a man had been at birth, but in the point he had reached, in what he had changed into, what he had become. In Shakespeare's view, Othello, who was black, was a human being and a Christian who lived in historic times, and this interested him the more because living side by side with Othello was Iago, who was white, and who was an unconverted prehistoric animal.

Antony and Cleopatra

There are tragedies in Shakespeare, such as *Macbeth* and *Lear*, which create their own worlds, unique of their kind. There are comedies which belong to the realm of pure fantasy and are the cradle of romanticism. There are chronicles of English history, songs in praise of England sung by the greatest of her sons; some of the events described in them had their counterpart in the circumstances of his time and so his attitude to them could not be sober and dispassionate.

Thus, in spite of the realism in which his work is steeped, it would be vain to look to any of these plays for objectivity. We do, however, find it in his dramas of Roman life.

Julius Caesar was not written only for the sake of poetry and love of art, and still less was *Antony and Cleopatra.* Both are the fruit of his study of plain everyday life. This study is pursued with passion by every representational artist. It was this pursuit which led to the naturalistic novel of the nineteenth century and which accounts for the even more convincing charm of Flaubert, Chekhov, and Leo Tolstoy.

But why should Shakespeare seek the inspiration of his realism in such remote antiquity as Rome? The answer—and there is nothing in it to surprise us— is that just because the subject was remote it allowed Shakespeare to call things by their name. He could say whatever seemed good to him about politics, ethics, or any other thing he chose. He was dealing with an alien and distant world, a world which had long since ceased to exist and was closed, accounted for, and passive. What desire could it arouse? He wished to portray it.

Antony and Cleopatra is the story of a rake and a

temptress. In describing them as they burn up their lives Shakespeare uses the tones of mystery fitting to a genuine bacchanalia in the classical sense.

Historians have written that neither Antony nor Cleopatra (nor his companions in his feasts, nor the courtiers who were in her confidence) expected any good to come of the debauchery which they had promoted to the status of a ritual. Foreseeing the end, they spoke of themselves, long before it came, as immortal suicides and promised to die together.

This indeed is the conclusion of the tragedy. At the decisive moment death is the draftsman who lends the story the connecting outline which it had so far lacked. Against the background of campaigns, fires, treason, and defeats, we take leave on two separate occasions of the two principal characters. In the fourth act the hero stabs himself, and the heroine commits suicide in the fifth.

The Audience

Shakespeare's chronicles of English history abound in hints at the topical events of his day. There were no newspapers: to hear the news (as G. B. Harrison notes in his *England in Shakespeare's Day*) people gathered in taverns and theaters. Drama spoke in hints. Nor is it surprising that the common people understood them since they concerned facts which were close to everyone.

The political open secret of the time was the difficulties of the war with Spain, started with enthusiasm but which had soon become a bore. For fifteen years it had been waged by land and sea, off the coast of Portugal and in the Netherlands and in Ireland.

Falstaff's parodies of martial speeches amused the simple, peaceful public, which plainly understood what was meant, and which laughed still more heartily at his recruiting scene (where the recruits bribe their way out) because it knew the truth of it by experience.

A great deal more astonishing is another example of the intelligence of the contemporary audience.

The works of Shakespeare, as of all Elizabethans, are full of appeals to history and ancient literature and of mythological examples and names. To understand them nowadays, even reference book in hand, one needs to be a classical scholar; yet we are told that the average Londoner of those days caught these flickering allusions in mid-air and digested them without the least trouble. How are we to believe this?

The explanation is that the school curriculum was very different from ours. A knowledge of Latin, which is now taken for a sign of higher education, was then the lowest step to learning, just as Church Slavonic used to be in Russia. In the primary, so-called grammar schools—and Shakespeare went to one of them—Latin was the spoken language and, according to the historian Trevelyan, the schoolboys were not allowed to use English even in their games. Those London apprentices and shop assistants who could read and write were as much at home with Fortune, Heracles, and Niobe as a modern schoolboy with internal combustion and the elements of electricity.

Shakespeare was born in time to find a well-established, century-old way of life still in being. His age was a festive period in England's history. By the end of the next reign the balance of things had already been upset.

Authenticity of Shakespeare's Authorship

Shakespeare's work is a whole and he is everywhere true to himself. He is recognizable by his vocabulary. Certain of his characters appear under different names in play after play and he sings the same song over and over to different tunes. His habit of repeating and paraphrasing himself is particularly noticeable in *Hamlet*.

In a scene with Horatio, Hamlet tells him that he is a man and cannot be played upon like a pipe.

A few pages further on he asks Guildenstern, in the same allegorical sense, whether he would like to play the pipe.

In the first player's monologue about the cruelty of Fortune in allowing Priam to be killed, the gods are urged to punish her by breaking her wheel, the symbol of her power, and flinging the pieces down from heaven to Tartarus. A few pages further on, Rosencrantz, speaking to the King, compares a monarch's power to a wheel fixed on a mount which, if its foundations are shaken, destroys everything on its way as it hurtles down.

Juliet takes the dagger from dead Romeo's side and stabs herself with the words "This is thy sheath." A few lines further on her father uses the same words about the dagger resting in Juliet's breast instead of in the sheath on Romeo's belt. And so on, almost at every step. What does this mean?

Translating Shakespeare is a task which takes time and effort. Once it is undertaken, it is best to divide it into sections long enough for the work not to get stale and to complete one section each day. In thus daily progressing through the text, the translator finds himself reliving the circumstances of the author. Day by day he reproduces his actions and he is drawn into some of his secrets, not in theory but practically, by experience.

Stumbling on such repetitions as I have mentioned and realizing how close together they are, he cannot help asking himself in surprise: "Who and in what conditions would remember so little of what he had put down only a few days earlier?"

Then, with a tangible certainty which is not given to the biographer or the scholar, the translator becomes aware of the personality of Shakespeare and of his genius. In twenty years Shakespeare wrote thirty-six plays, not to speak of his poems and sonnets. Forced to write two plays a year on an average, he had no time to revise and, constantly forgetting what he had written the day before, he repeated himself in his hurry.

At this point the absurdity of the Baconian theory becomes more striking than ever. What need was there to replace the simple and in no way improbable account of Shakespeare's life by a tangle of mysterious substitutions and their alleged discoveries?

Is it conceivable that Rutland, Bacon, or Southampton should have disguised himself so unsuccessfully; that, using a cypher or a faked identity, he should have hidden from Elizabeth and her time only to reveal himself so carelessly to later generations? What cunning, what ulterior purpose can be imagined in the mind of this highly reckless man who undoubtedly existed, who was not ashamed of slips of the pen, and who, yawning with fatigue in the face of history, remembered less of his own work than any high school pupil knows of it today? His strength shows itself in his weaknesses.

There is another puzzling thing. Why is it that ungifted people are so passionately interested in those who are great? They have their own conception of the artist, a conception which is idle, agreeable, and false. They start by assuming that Shakespeare was a genius in the sense in which they understand genius; they apply their yardstick to him and he fails to measure up to it.

His life, they find, was too obscure and workaday for his fame. He had no library of his own and his signature at the bottom of his will is a scrawl. It strikes them as suspicious that a man who knew the soil, the crops, the animals, and all the hours of the day and night as simple people know them should also have been at home with law, history, diplomacy, and the ways and habits of courtiers. And so they are astonished, amazed, forgetting that so great an artist must inevitably sum up everything human in himself.

King Henry IV

The period of Shakespeare's life about which there can be least doubt is his youth.

I am thinking of the time when he had just come to London as an unknown young provincial from Stratford. Probably he stayed for a while in the suburbs, further from the center of the town than a cabby would take his fare. Probably, out there, there was a sort of Yamskie village. With travellers to and from London stopping on their way, the place must have had something of the bustling life of a modern railway station; and there were probably lakes, woods, market gardens, stagecoach inns, booths, and amusement parks in the neighborhood. There may have been theaters. Smart people from London came to have a good time.

It was a world which had something about it of

the Tverskie-Yamskie of the middle of the last century when, on the outskirts of Moscow, beyond the river—surrounded by the nine muses and by lofty theories, troikas, publicans, gipsy choirs, and educated merchants who patronized the arts—lived and struggled the most distinguished Russian heirs of the young man from Stratford, Apollon Grigoryev and Ostrovsky.

The young man had no definite occupation but an unusually brilliant star. His belief in it had brought him to the capital. He did not yet know his future role, but his sense of life told him that he would play it unbelievably well.

Whatever he took up had been done before him: people had composed verses and plays, acted, obliged the visiting gentry, and tried as hard as they could to make their way in the world. But whatever this young man took up, he felt such an astonishing upsurge of strength that it was clearly best for him to break with all established habits and do everything in his own way.

Before him, only what was artificial and remote from life had been regarded as art. This artificiality was obligatory, and it was a convenient cloak for spiritual impotence and for inability to draw. But Shakespeare had so good an eye and so sure a hand that it was clearly to his advantage to upset the existing convention.

He realized how much he would gain if, instead of staying at the usual distance from life, he walked up to it—not on stilts but on his own legs—and, measuring himself against it, forced it to look down first before his stubbornly unblinking stare.

There was a company of actors, writers, and their patrons who went from pub to pub, baited strangers, and consistently risked their necks by laughing at everything in the world. The most reckless of them, who yet remained unharmed (he got away with everything), the least moderate and the most sober (drink never went to his head), the one who raised the loudest laugh and who was yet the most reserved, was this gloomy youth who was already striding into the future in his seven-league boots.

Perhaps there really was a fat old Falstaff who went about with these young people. Or perhaps Shakespeare invented him later as an embodiment of that time.

It was not only as a gay memory that it became dear to him: this was the time which saw the birth of Shakespeare's realism. It was not in the solitude of his study that he conceived it but in the early hours in an unmade room in an inn, a room as charged with life as a gun with powder. Shakespeare's realism is not the profundity of a reformed rake nor the hackneyed "wisdom" of later experience. That which is most earnest, grave, tragic, and essential in his art arose out of his consciousness of success and strength in those wild early days of desperate fooling, inventiveness, and hourly mortal danger.

King Lear

The productions of *King Lear* are always too noisy. There is the willful, obstinate old man, there are the gatherings in the echoing palace hall, shouts, orders, and afterwards curses and sobs of despair merging with the rolls of thunder and the noises of the wind. But in fact, the only stormy thing in the play is the tempest at night, while the people, huddled in the tent and terrified, speak in whispers.

Lear is as quiet as *Romeo,* and for the same reason. In *Romeo* it is the love of lovers which is persecuted and in hiding; in *Lear* it is filial love and, more widely, the love of one's neighbor, the love of truth.

Only the criminals in *King Lear* wield the notions of duty and honor; they alone are sensible and eloquent, and logic and reason assist them in their frauds, cruelties, and murders. All the decent people are either silent to the point of being indistinguishable from each other or make obscure and contradictory statements which lead to misunderstandings. The positive heroes are the fools, the madmen, the dying, and the vanquished.

Such is the content of this play written in the language of the Old Testament prophets and situated in a legendary epoch of pre-Christian barbarism.

Comedy and Tragedy in Shakespeare

There is no pure comedy or tragedy in Shakespeare. His style is between the two and made up of both; it is thus closer to the true face of life than either, for in life, too, horrors and delights are mixed. This has been accounted to him as a merit by all English critics, from Samuel Johnson to T. S. Eliot.

To Shakespeare, the difference between tragedy and comedy was not merely the difference between the lofty and the commonplace, the ideal and the real. He used them rather as the major and minor keys in music. In arranging his material he employed poetry and prose and the transitions from one to the other as variations in music.

These transitions are the chief characteristic of his dramatic art; they are at the very heart of his stage-craft and they convey that hidden rhythm of thought and mood which I referred to in my note on *Hamlet.*

All his dramas are made up of swiftly alternating scenes of tragedy and tomfoolery. One aspect of this method is particularly marked.

On the edge of Ophelia's grave the audience is made to laugh at the philosophizing of the grave-diggers. At the moment when Juliet's corpse is carried out, the boy from the servants' hall giggles at the musicians who have been invited to a wedding, and the musicians bargain with the nurse who is trying to get rid of them. Cleopatra's suicide is preceded by the appearance of the half-wit Egyptian snake-charmer with his absurd reflections on the uselessness of reptiles—almost as in Maeterlinck or in Leonid Andreyev!

Shakespeare was the father and the prophet of realism. His influence on Pushkin, Victor Hugo, and other poets is well known. He was studied by the German romantics. One of the Schlegels translated him into German and the other drew on him for his theory of romantic irony. Goethe, as the symbolist author of *Faust,* was his descendant. Finally, to keep only to the essentials, as a dramatist he is the predecessor of Chekhov and of Ibsen.

It is in this same spirit, which he transmitted to his heirs, that he makes vulgar mediocrity snort and rush in on the funereal solemnity of his finales.

Its irruption makes the mystery of death, already inaccessibly remote from us, withdraw still further. The respectful distance we keep between ourselves and the threshold of what is lofty and frightening grows a little longer still. No situation as seen by the artist or the thinker is final; every position is the last but one. It is as if Shakespeare were afraid lest the audience should believe too firmly in the seemingly unconditional finality of his dénouements. By breaking up the rhythm at the end he re-establishes infinity. In keeping with the character of modern art and in contrast to the fatalism of the ancient world, he dissolves the mortal, temporal quality of the individual sign in its immortal, universal significance.

Macbeth

Macbeth might well have been called *Crime and Punishment*. All the time I was translating it I was haunted by its likeness to Dostoevsky's novel.

Planning the murder of Banquo, Macbeth tells his hired murderers:

Your spirits shine through you. Within this hour at
    most
I will advise you where to plant yourselves,
Acquaint you with the perfect spy o' the time,
The moment on't; for 't must be done tonight,
And something from the palace . . .

A little further on, in the third scene of the third act, the murderers, lying in ambush for Banquo, watch the guests arriving through the park.

SECOND MURDERER:

                  Then 'tis he: the rest
    That are within the note of expectation
    Already are i' the court.

FIRST MURDERER:

                 His horses go about.

THIRD MURDERER:

    Almost a mile: but he does usually—
    So all men do—from hence to the palace gate
    Make it their walk . . .

Murder is a desperate, dangerous business. Everything must be thought out, every possibility must be foreseen. Both Shakespeare and Dostoevsky endow their heroes with their own foresight and imagination, their own capacities for timeliness, detail, and precision. Both the novel and the play have the sharp, heightened realism of detection and of detective fiction: the cautious wariness of the policeman who looks over his shoulder as often as the criminal himself.

Neither Macbeth nor Raskolnikov is a born criminal or a villain by nature. They are turned into criminals by faulty rationalizations, by deductions from false premises.

In one case the impetus is given by the prophecy of the witches who set the vanity of Macbeth ablaze. In the other, it comes from the extreme nihilistic proposition that, if there is no God, everything is allowed, and therefore a murder is in no way different from any other human act.

Of the two, Macbeth feels particularly safe from retribution. What could threaten him? A forest walking across a plain? A man not born of woman?—Such things don't exist, they are blatant absurdities. In other words, he may shed blood fearlessly. And what, in any case, has he to fear from justice once he has seized kingly power and become the only source of law? It all seems so clear and logical! What could be more simple and obvious? And so the crimes follow in quick succession—many crimes over a long time—until the forest suddenly moves and sets out on its way and an avenger comes who is not born of woman.

Incidentally, about Lady Macbeth—coolness and will power are not her predominant qualities. I think that what is strongest in her is something more generally feminine. She is one of those active, insistent wives, a woman who is her husband's helper, his support, for whom her husband's interests are her own and who takes his plans on faith once and for all. She neither discusses them nor judges nor selects among them. To reason, to doubt, to make plans—that's her husband's business, it's his lookout. She is his executive, more resolute and consistent than he is himself. Miscalculating her strength, she assumes the excessive burden and is destroyed, not by conscience but by spiritual exhaustion, sadness, and fatigue.

NOTES
—

An alphabetical list of names mentioned in the text, with the exception of names of internationally known writers.

ACMEISM. Movement in Russian poetry founded in 1912 as a reaction against symbolism. The acmeists objected to the mysticism and vagueness of symbolist poetry and called for a return to clarity, precision, and concreteness. They also emphasized the virile and heroic aspects of life.

AKHMATOVA, pseudonym of Anna Arkadyevna Gorenko (1888–   ). Poet. Began to publish poetry in 1907. Love lyrics published in 1912–15 established her popularity. After the Revolution she published one book in 1923, *A.D. 1921,* then fell silent; after a gap of seventeen years, published another book of poems in 1940. Married to Gumilyov, whom she divorced in 1918. During her long period of silence as a poet, she published some important studies of Pushkin. In 1940 she took advantage of the greater leniency of the war years to publish a selection of her poems, new and old. Zhdanov launched an attack on her in 1946 which led to her expulsion from the Union of Soviet Writers. In 1950 she published a number of patriotic verses of rather poor quality. Her poems show some of the best qualities of acmeism. Her range of subject matter is small, concerned chiefly with the themes of love and death, treated with a tinge of mysticism reminiscent of symbolism. Her works show no marked development of style or ideas.

ALKONOST. Publishers of Blok's works. Volume II of this edition appeared in 1922, in Petersburg. Alkonost—from Russian folk tales: a fairyland bird with a human face.

ANDREYEVA, MARIA FYODOROVNA (1872–1953). Actress. Joined Stanislavsky's amateur theatrical group in 1894 and afterwards became a member of the Moscow Art Theater. Stanislavsky admired her as a "Gothic" actress. Played Irina in *The Three Sisters*, Varya in *The Cherry Orchard*, Natasha in *The Lower Depths*, etc. Joined Marxist student organization. From 1903 associated with Gorky, acting as his secretary. Visited a number of European countries and the U.S.A. along with Gorky, 1906. Accompanied Gorky to London in 1907. Returned to the stage in 1913. Helped to establish Petersburg Bolshoi Theater in 1919, acting in it 1919–26. From 1931 to 1948 was Director of Moscow Scientists' and Scholars' Club.

ANNENSKY, INNOKENTY FYODOROVICH (1856–1909). Symbolist poet. Tried to introduce the impressionism of Verlaine and Mallarmé into Russia. Translator of Euripides, Rimbaud, and Baudelaire. First appeared in print as writer of reviews and articles on educational subjects in the 1880's. In 1904 published a book of lyric poems, *Quiet Songs,* under the pseudonym Nik-to (*nikto*—nobody). His second book of poems, *The Cypress Chest,* was published posthumously in 1910. Tried to depict the world of the "sick soul," described nightmares, etc. His verse became known long before his death in the circle around the journal *Apollon,* then was forgotten. Revived interest in him about 1923.

Apollon. A symbolist review.

ASEYEV, NIKOLAI NIKOLAYEVICH (1889–   ). Poet. Began writing symbolist poetry in 1913. Met Mayakovsky and much influenced by him. Published collections of verse during the First World War. During Civil War published revolutionary verses. In 1923 was one of the founders of the journal *Lef*. Notable poems on revolutionary themes: *The 26* (i.e., the 26 Baku Commissars executed in 1918) (1926). Poem in honor of Mayakovsky awarded Stalin Prize, 1941. Aseyev tries to distinguish Mayakovsky sharply from such futurists as Khlebnikov. During the 1941–45 war wrote patriotic verses, and after the war wrote anti-American verses and songs.

BABEL, ISAAK EMANUILOVICH (1894–1938). Outstanding Soviet short-story writer. Born in Odessa, Jewish; his first stories were published by Gorky in his *Annals* in 1915. They were highly erotic, and Babel was prosecuted for pornography. Took part in the Polish campaign with Budyony's Cossack cavalry. His short stories of the early Soviet period began to appear in 1923 and he was immediately recognized as an outstanding writer. His stories are stories of blood and death, of cold-blooded crime, of heroism and cruelty. There is always a grain of irony in them which does not destroy but only enhances the heroic pathos. They deal with the Polish campaign (*The Red Cavalry,* 1923) and with the Odessa underworld. (Probably killed in the purge of

1937–38. His stories were republished in Russia and his work discussed for the first time since 1937 in 1956.)

BAGRITSKY, EDUARD GEORGIEVICH, pseudonym of Dzubin (1895–1934). Poet. Born in Odessa; Jewish. Wrote verses during First World War under influence of Gumilyov and acmeism. Verses written in the 1920's deal with Civil War themes and with life of fishermen and sailors. The setting of his major work, *The Epic of Apanas,* 1926, is the Civil War of the Ukraine. Poems written in the 1930's hail the constructive labor of ordinary people (*The New Knights*) and especially the Soviet young generation (*Death of a Pioneer Girl*).

BALMONT, KONSTANTIN DMITRIEVICH (1867–1943). Poet. Leader of early symbolist movement in Russia. Collections of poems: *Under the Northern Light* (1894); *Shoreless* (1895); *Silence* (1898); *Burning Building* (1900); *Let's Be Like the Sun* (1903); *Liturgy of Beauty* (1905); *Evil Charms* (1906); *Bird of Flame* (1906). Travelled in South Africa, Mexico, New Zealand, Spain. Translated Shelley, Whitman, Poe, and Calderón. Emigrated in 1918 and died in Paris.

BALTRUSHAITIS, JURGIS (1873–1945). Poet. Born in a Lithuanian peasant family. Wrote poetry from 1899 onward, in both Russian and Lithuanian. Associated with the symbolists, and one of the founders of their publishing house Skorpion. Distinguished as translator of Byron, Ibsen, D'Annunzio, Hamsun, Wilde, and Strindberg.

BELINSKY, VISSARION GRIGORYEVICH (1811–48). Famous Russian literary critic, who has greatly influenced Russian contemporary writings. A close friend of Turgenev.

Was the first literary critic to appreciate Dostoevsky's genius.

BELY, ANDREY, pseudonym of Bugayev, Boris Nikolayevich (1880–1934). Poet and novelist. One of the principal representatives of Russian symbolism. Born in Moscow, son of a professor of mathematics. Studied in Moscow. In 1904 began to contribute to Bryusov's journal *Vessy* (Scales) and soon became one of the most outstanding theoreticians of symbolism, which he conceived not merely as a literary school but as a world outlook. Became a follower of Rudolf Steiner, the anthroposophist, in 1912. His first writings appeared in 1902 under the title *Symphony (Second, Dramatic)*, followed by the *First* (1904), *Third* (1905), and *Fourth* "Symphonies." Most famous of his prose works is his novel *Petersburg*. He is also the author of works on the history of literature. Recognized as a master of meter and rhythm, some of his works being written in rhythmic, musical prose.

BLOK, ALEXANDER ALEXANDROVICH (1880–1921). Greatest Russian poet of modern times. Began publishing verses in 1903. Contributed to symbolist journal *The Golden Fleece*, as poet, playwright, and critic. Served in the army during the First World War. After the Revolution, worked in the Commission for Publishing the Classics, and in the theatrical section of the Commissariat of Education. His early poems are full of mysticism and the sense of impending catastrophe. In his first poems, *Verses About a Beautiful Woman*, he gives an ideal picture of a woman who is the incarnation of the "eternal feminine." The 1905 Revolution made a big impression on him, and after that he wrote on social themes, such as the contrasts and antagonisms of rich and poor, etc. He greeted the October Revolution as a cleansing storm. He entered the Soviet poetic scene with his great poem *The Twelve,* an apocalyptic vision of the Revolution, personified in twelve Red Army men as the apostles of the new world, headed by Christ crowned with a wreath of white roses, and marching invisible and unscathed through the raging storm. In the same period *The Scythians* (1918) expresses Russia's "love-hatred" for the West.

BLUE ROSE, THE. Name given to a Moscow art exhibition of 1907, the participants in which were decorative impressionists.

BOBROV, SERGEY PAVLOVICH (1881–). Futurist poet, and author of works on versification and the theory of literature. Also prose writer: *The Uprising of the Misanthropes,* a fantasy of world revolution.

BRYUSOV, VALERY YAKOVLEVICH (1873–1924). One of the founders of the symbolist movement in Russia. Born in Moscow. His grandfather and father were serfs who later became small tradesmen. Educated in private schools and Moscow University, where he studied philosophy. He provides a living link between Soviet poetry and the great Russian poetry of the past. At the age of twenty-two, in 1895 he issued his manifesto to the world: "Incapable of entreaties and tears, I have locked my door and cursed our days." These first poems, published in *Russian Symbolists,* made him famous. Followed it up with two more volumes, *Chef*

NOTES

d'oeuvre (1894–95) and *Me Eum Esse* (1896–97). The hero of his lyric poems is a militant individualist, an enemy of materialism. He was much influenced by Baudelaire and Verlaine. The chief aim of symbolism, according to the young Bryusov, was to make his readers see the world in a new light and stimulate their imaginations. By 1903 he was the recognized head of the symbolist movement. He edited the symbolist review *Vessy* (Scales) from 1904 to 1909. During the First World War acted as war correspondent of a Moscow paper. Author of several plays as well as translations of plays performed on the Petersburg and Moscow stages. After the October Revolution he rallied to the new regime, and did much to instruct the young Soviet poets in the art of poetry.

CHIKOVANI, SIMON IVANOVICH (1902–   ). Soviet poet glorifying benefits of Revolution in Georgia. Awarded the Stalin Prize in 1947.

CONSTRUCTIVISTS. Group of poets formed in 1924 around Selvinsky. From the futurists they took their interest in technology and other contemporary themes, but they were not so antitraditional. Their central idea was that all the images and devices of a poem must be directed toward the poem's subject: e.g., a poem about war should have a marching rhythm. The group broke up in 1930.

D'ALHEIM OLENINA, MARIA ALEXEYEVNA (1871–   ). Mezzo-soprano. Made her debut in Paris in 1897 at Musorgsky concerts. First performed in Russia in 1901. Founded the music society Dom Pesni (The House of

Song) in 1908 in Moscow. This played a notable role in development of musical taste in Moscow and Petersburg. Wrote a book, *The Legacy of Musorgsky*. After 1918 lived in Paris. Married to the French critic Pierre D'Alheim, who did much to make Musorgsky's music known in France.

DONKEY'S TAIL, THE. Name assumed by a group of surrealist painters.

DROZHZHIN, SPIRIDON DMITRIEVICH (1848–1930). Poet, of peasant origin. Began publishing verse 1873. From 1896 lived in his native village in Tver province, occupied with farming and writing. Wrote verse depicting the hard life of the peasants. Much influenced by Nekrasov. Welcomed the October Revolution and wrote verse in its honor, notably *In Memory of Lenin*, 1924.

DURYLIN, SERGEY NIKOLAYEVICH (1881–   ). Poet. Pseudonyms: S. Severny, S. Rayevsky. Best known for his writings about literature. Early works much influenced by symbolism. In 1916 wrote a study of the poet Lermontov, examining his verses from the standpoint of Andrey Bely's theories. Important later books: *Repin and Garshin*, 1926, *From Gogol's Family Chronicle*, 1928, *About Tolstoy*, 1928.

EHRENBURG, ILYA GEORGIEVICH (1891–   ). Poet and novelist. Left Russia in 1909 for Paris, where he entered the Bohemian literary world. His first poetry appeared in 1911. During the First World War remained in France as war correspondent. Returned to Russia in 1917, and lived in the South, under the Whites. In 1921 was arrested by the Soviet authorities, but released on "accepting" the Revolution. Returned to Paris and spent most of his time in the West until 1941. Was Soviet war correspondent in Spain in 1936–37. During Second World War wrote much patriotic propaganda. First successful novel, *Julio Jurenito,* 1922, satirical and cynical. *Trust D.E.,* 1923, a fantasy of the conquest of Europe by America. *The Second Day,* 1933, depicts the construction of a steel works in Siberia. His *Storm* and *The Ninth Wave* were translated into English and widely read in England and America. His latest novel, *The Thaw,* met with violent attacks in Soviet Russia and involved him in heated polemics with several writers, especially Konstantin Simonov. He is now under a cloud.

ELLIS-KOBYLINSKY, LEV LVOVICH (1874–1947). Poet and critic. Member of the Society of Religious Philosophy. Emigrated and died in Locarno.

ENGEL, YURI DMITRIEVICH (1868–1927). Studied at Moscow Conservatory. From 1897 in charge of the music column in *Russkyie Vyedomosti.* One of the founders of the People's Conservatory, 1906, and of the Society for Jewish Folk Music, 1908. First biographer of Scriabin. After October Revolution active in musical education work for the schools. After 1924 lived at Tel-Aviv.

ESENIN, SERGEY ALEXANDROVICH (1895–1925). One of the greatest modern Russian lyric poets. Son of a peasant. Worked in Moscow as a proofreader. Influenced by Blok and Bely. Equally unsurpassable as a nature poet and as a poet of love lyrics; in both nature and love he depicted the eternally true and the eternally different. The peculiar charm of his poetry is its freshness. Joined the imagists and led a rowdy café life with them. Married the famous dancer, Isadora Duncan, in 1922 and went abroad with her, but they separated and he returned to Russia in 1923. Suffered a mental collapse in 1925, wrote a farewell poem in his own blood, and hanged himself.

FADEYEV, ALEXANDER ALEXANDROVICH (1901–56). Novelist. Of peasant origin, grew up in Far Eastern Siberia. Served on the Red side in the Civil War. His first important work was his short novel *The Rout,* 1927, set among the partisans of the Far East. Another novel, *The Last of the Udegs,* 1928–36, depicts the changes brought about by the Revolution in the life of an almost extinct Far Eastern tribe. In 1939 he was made Secretary of the Union of Soviet Writers. In 1945 he wrote *The Young Guard,* a war novel. He rewrote sections of this novel after strong Communist Party criticism. Committed suicide in 1956 after a strongly worded attack on him by Sholokhov, who accused him of having been corrupted by his "love of power," at the Communist Party Congress.

FEDIN, KONSTANTIN ALEXANDROVICH (1892–). Prominent Russian novelist. A member of the Serapion group. Published *The Orchard* in 1920, which was attacked by Soviet critics. His first novel, *Cities and Years,* 1924, was one of the earliest attempts to depict the impact of the Revolution on an intellectual. Soviet critics accused Fedin of sharing his hero's "doubts." His second novel, *Brothers,* 1928, deals with the mission of the artist, whose right to individualism is opposed to the obligations of Soviet life, and again Fedin seemed to sympathize with his nonconforming hero. In the 1930's Fedin appears to have overcome his objections to the Soviet regime. *The Rape of Europe,* 1934–35, contrasts "decadent" Western Europe with progressive Russia. His postwar novels, *Early Joys,* 1945–46, and *Extraordinary Summer,* 1948, are his best work.

FIELD, JOHN (1782–1837). Composer and pianist. Born in Dublin and settled in Moscow. Chopin used his nocturnes as models.

FUTURISM. Poetry movement founded in 1910 by Khlebnikov. A manifesto published by him, Mayakovsky, and others in 1912 was entitled *A Slap in the Face of Public Taste.* In revolt against symbolism, especially against its mysticism and aestheticism, the futurists were fascinated by the most modern features of modern life. They wanted to scrap the whole cultural tradition of the past and to wake everybody up by shock methods. In 1923 they formed an organization and a journal called *Lef* (Left Front) to oppose the tendency toward a return to conservative realism. They did not have much success, and the journal closed down in 1925. A new *Lef* was begun in 1927, but it, too, soon ceased publication.

GE, NIKOLAY NIKOLAYEVICH (1831–94). Russian painter. Studied in Italy. His paintings on themes from the New Testament show remarkable psychological insight and dramatic power. On return to Petersburg in 1869 was active in *Peredvizhniki* group. Historical paintings, notably *Peter the Great with the Tsarevich*

Alexey (1871); portraits of Turgenev, Antokolsky, Saltykov-Shchedrin, Nekrasov, and other eminent contemporaries. Left Petersburg to live in the country and painted a series of scenes from the life of Christ. Fell under the influence of Tolstoy, whose portrait he painted in 1884.

GLIER, REINHOLD MORITSOVICH (1874–   ). Composer. Born in Kiev of a musical family. Studied music in Kiev and at Moscow Conservatory. Began conducting, 1908. In 1914–20 director of Kiev Conservatory. In 1920–41 director of Moscow Conservatory. Already known for his symphonies before the Revolution, Glier's best period began after it. He was one of the first composers of the older generation to rally to the Soviet regime and help it in its educational and cultural work. His *Red Poppy* (1927) was the first ballet on a contemporary revolutionary theme. He devoted special attention to the folk music of Azerbaijan and Central Asia and composed operas based on their folk-lore. Prokofiev, Myaskovsky, and several other famous composers studied under Glier.

Golden Fleece, The. A monthly review (1906–09) of the symbolists of the second generation, including Blok.

GOLITZIN, DMITRI PETROVICH, PRINCE (1860–1919). Published tales, novels, and poems under the pseudonym of Muravlin. Influenced by Dostoevsky.

GOLITZIN, NIKOLAY DMITRIEVICH, PRINCE (1850–1925). Last chairman of the Tsar's council of ministers, 1916–17.

GONCHAROVA, NATALYA SERGEYEVNA (1883–   ). Painter. Studied under Trubetskoy in Moscow, 1899–1902. As artist, fell under influence of most "extreme" tendencies of her time, such as cubism, etc., 1911–13. Futurist pictures include *Airplane over a Train*. Growing interest in Eastern folk art; influence of Henri Rousseau. Together with Larionov, whom she married, tried to found a new theory, *Luchism* (*Luch*—"ray"), related to cubism, but nothing came of this. In later works, e.g., *Spanish Girls,* Goncharova tried to combine the traditions of the great painters of the West with the methods of ancient Russian fresco painters. Participated in *World of Art* exhibitions. Went to Paris on Diaghilev's invitation, and was responsible for sets for a number of his productions, such as *Le Coq d'Or* and others. Exhibited in Paris and America.

GRIN, ALEXANDER STEPANOVICH, pseudonym of Grinevsky (1890–1932). Author of fantastic novels and stories.

GUMILYOV, NIKOLAY STEPANOVICH (1886–1921). Poet and critic. Educated at the Sorbonne and at Petersburg University. Travelled in Abyssinia and Somaliland. Served as volunteer in 1914 war. Fought on the Salonika front. Went to France after the February Revolution, became Provisional Government Commissioner for the affairs of Russian troops in France. In 1918 returned to Russia. Shot in 1921 for alleged participation in White Guard conspiracy. As poet, Gumilyov began under the influence of the symbolists. Following Bryusov, he wrote about exotic, savage countries: *The Giraffe*. He then became the leader of the acmeist group. After the October Revolution he returned to symbolism and mysticism. His best works are *The Pyre*, 1918, and *The Pillar of Fire*, 1921. Translated Théophile Gautier.

HAMSUN, KNUT, pseudonym of Knut Pedersen (1859–1952). Norwegian novelist. His novel *Hunger,* published in 1890, in which he described irrational processes in the mind of a starving man in a lyric ecstatic style influenced by Dostoevsky, made him famous. Wrote a trilogy, 1906–09–12, about a vagabond dreamer. A neo-romantic individualist in revolt against civilization. His *Growth of the Soil,* 1917, was an epic of the simple life for which he was awarded the Nobel Prize. His novels were very popular in Russia, and at one time he was read more avidly there than Ibsen. His extremely reactionary views led to collaboration with the Nazi occupiers of Norway. He was tried for treason after the war and fined the greater part of his fortune.

IMAGISTS. A group of Moscow poets whose theory was that the principal thing in poetry is "imagery." Their poetry is therefore an agglomeration of "images" of the most far-fetched and exaggerated description. They made it a special point not to distinguish between "pure" and "impure," and to introduce the coarsest and crudest images side by side with the pathetic and the sublime. The group was founded in 1919 and fell apart after 1924.

IVANOV, SERGEY VASILYEVICH (1846–1910). A genre painter and a member of the Society for Travelling Art Exhibitions.

IVANOV, VSEVOLOD VYACHESLAVICH (1895–   ). Soviet novelist and playwright. Was actor, sailor, printshopworker. Took part in Civil War in Siberia and wrote stories about it: *Partisans,* 1921. His play *Armored Train 14-69* (1922) was produced by Stanislavsky for the Moscow Art Theater in 1927. Associated for a time with the Serapion Fraternity. Another play of his, *Blockade* (1929), deals with the suppression of the Baltic Fleet mutiny in Kronstadt in 1921. At the end of the 1930's returned to Civil War themes and wrote the novel *Parkhomenko* (1938–39), about one of the heroes of the Red Army. In addition, wrote patriotic articles and tales during the 1941–45 war, and in 1947 published *Encounters with Maxim Gorky.*

IVANOV, VYACHESLAV IVANOVICH (1866–1949). Symbolist poet. Appointed professor of Greek at Baku in 1921. In 1924 left the Soviet Union on an official mission. Remained in Italy, becoming a convert to Roman Catholicism. In *Guiding Stars,* a book of poetry published in 1903, he proclaimed the equation of Christ and Dionysos. According to him, "ecstasy for ecstasy's sake" was to be found in "symphonic" culture and nonacceptance of the world.

JACK OF DIAMONDS, THE (1910–26). Name of a group of formalist painters hostile to realism in painting.

KHLEBNIKOV, VELEMIR (Viktor Vladimirovich) (1886–1922). Experimental poet. His first verses (1906–08) showed the influence of symbolism, but later he became connected with the futurists and went in for word-creation. He idealized the patriarchal past of the Slavs. He hailed the October Revolution, which, however, he conceived as a sort of "Stenka Razin" affair, an elemental revolt. In his last poems he attempted a fantastic picture of the society of the future. Mayakovsky admired Khlebnikov's experimental efforts. Russian futurism dates from 1910, when Khlebnikov published his famous etymological poem, which was nothing but a series of freshly coined derivatives of one word, *smekh* (laughter).

KHODASEVICH, VLADISLAV FELITSIANOVICH (1886-1939). Poet. First volume of symbolist poems, *Youth,* published in 1908. Fascinated by death, disintegration, and monstrosity. A successor to Annensky. In exile from 1922. His latest poems (*The Way of the Grain,* 1920, and *The Heavy Lyre,* 1923) show a return to the Russian classical traditions.

KLEIST, HEINRICH WILHELM VON (1777-1811). German poet and playwright, associated with Goethe, Schiller, and Wieland. Most important North German dramatist of the romantic movement. Lived mainly in Berlin. Infatuated with a woman of brilliant musical talent and died in a suicide pact with her.

KLYUCHEVSKY, VASILY OSIPOVICH (1841-1911). Professor of history at Moscow University. A right-wing liberal. His most important work was his *Course of Russian History,* in five volumes, published between 1904 and 1911.

KOLTSOV, ALEXEY VASILYEVICH (1809-42). Poet. Born in Voronezh in a cattle merchant's family. Had a hard childhood, spent only two years at the parish school. His father tried to suppress the boy's literary aspirations. At sixteen, however, began to write verse. Dealt mainly with peasant life and the countryside—*The Forest,* 1838.

KOMMISSARZHEVSKAYA, VERA (1864-1910). Famous Russian dramatic actress. Began career in 1892 in amateur dramatics and a year later went to the provinces as a professional actress. In 1896 joined the Petersburg Alexandrinsky Theater and in 1902 left it for the provinces. Founded her own theater in Petersburg in 1904. Sister of famous producer Fyodor Kommissarzhevsky.

KOROVIN, KONSTANTIN ALEXEYEVICH (1861–1939). Landscape painter, but particularly famous as designer of scenery for the theater and opera, especially for productions of *A Life for the Tsar*, 1904, *Sadko*, 1906, *The Snow Maiden*, 1907, *Khovanshchina*, 1912. Later became impressionist. Died in exile.

KRYMOV, NIKOLAY PETROVICH (1884–   ). Painter. Studied in Moscow, 1904–11. Began as journalist, member of Blue Rose group. Later turned to realistic painting. Famous as a landscape painter—*A Summer Day, A Dull Day, Dawn in the Gorky Park of Culture and Rest*, 1937. Also did much theatrical scene designing.

Lef (Left-Wing Front). A left-wing literary journal of futurist writers published with interruptions from 1923 to 1930. Mayakovsky broke with *Lef* in 1928.

LEONIDZE, GEORGI NIKOLAYEVICH (1899–   ). Georgian poet. Studied at theological seminary and at Tiflis University. His first poems show influence of symbolists, but later he abandoned this school and wrote in honor of triumphs of socialist construction in Georgia—*To Lenin*, 1936. Also poems about the Georgian countryside and the history of Georgia. Awarded Stalin Prize for a poem about Stalin, 1941. Awarded further Stalin Prize in 1952.

LEVITAN, ISAAK ILYICH (1860–1900). One of the most famous Russian landscape painters and one of Anton Chekhov's closest friends. Studied in Moscow in 1884 under Polenov. His famous series of scenes along the Volga painted in the 1880's and 1890's. Some of his works have indirect social and political criticism—e.g., *Vladimirka* (1892), showing the road along which exiles to Siberia were taken. Taught in Moscow from 1898. In 1889 visited Paris, where he discovered the Barbizon painters and impressionists, whose style he assimilated.

LOMONOSOV, MIKHAIL VASILYEVICH (1711–65). Poet and scientist. Son of a peasant, born near Archangel. Walked to Moscow in 1730 in search of an education, living in very difficult circumstances. Attracted attention by his outstanding abilities. Taken into the secondary school attached to the Academy of Sciences. In 1736 sent to Germany to study chemistry and metallurgy. Was at Marburg University, 1736–40, where he married. Travelled in Germany and Holland. Returned to Russia, 1741. Given a post in the Academy of Sciences. In 1745 made professor of chemistry; in 1757 put in charge of the Academy's Geographical Department. Later became head of Moscow University. Author of important works on physics and chemistry. Also distinguished as a poet. Called "the father of modern Russian literature." Wrote an important *Letter on the Rules of Russian Versification,* and works on Russian grammar and style.

MAKOVSKY, SERGEY KONSTANTINOVICH (1878–   ). Poet, critic, and editor of Petersburg review *Apollon* (1909–17). Emigrated in 1922, living in Paris.

MAKOVSKY, VLADIMIR YEGOROVICH (1846–1920). Painter,

member of the Society for Travelling Art Exhibitions. Prominent in realist revolt against academicism. Paintings of urban life in which emphasis is laid on social contrasts and sympathy shown for the poor and the oppressed. His pictures include *The Condemned*, 1879, *Bank Crash*, 1881, *Examination of a Revolutionary*, 1904.

MANDELSTAM, OSIP EMILIEVICH (1892–1938). An acmeist poet associated with Gumilyov and Akhmatova. First poem published in *Apollon* in 1910. Influenced by French classical poets. First book of poems, entitled *Kamen* (Stone), appeared in 1913. Another volume of poems, *Tristia,* published in 1922. Between 1920 and 1926 published three books of children's poems and translations from French and English prose. Own prose works include a book of essays, *On Poetry*, 1928, *The Noise of Time*, 1925, and *The Egyptian Stamp*, 1928. His last known original poems include the cycle *Armenia, Leningrad,* and *Midnight in Moscow*. Bitterly opposed to Bolshevism, and in 1932, at an informal gathering at the Moscow apartment of Boris Pasternak, recited a satirical piece derogatory to Stalin. Some days later arrested and banished. Released in 1937, but soon arrested again and believed to have died in Vladivostok hospital in December, 1938.

MANIFESTO OF OCTOBER 17, 1905. The Tsar issued a manifesto promising a constitution, and a procession of students carrying Red flags was attacked by Cossacks, on this day. One of the students was killed. His funeral procession a few days later turned into a mass demonstration by students and workers. The same evening

Cossacks and the reactionary, terroristic Black Hundreds beat and killed a number of students.

MARIA ALEXEVNA, PRINCESS. A fictitious character mentioned in Griboyedov's famous comedy, *The Misfortune of Being Clever*. The Russian Mrs. Grundy.

MARTYNOV, LEONID NIKOLAYEVICH (1905–   ). Poet and journalist. Travelled in Siberia and Central Asia. From 1922 on, published poems about those parts, especially on Civil War themes.

MAYAKOVSKY, VLADIMIR VLADIMIROVICH (1893–1930). Famous Soviet poet. Studied painting and came under futurist influence. Signed futurist manifesto in 1912. In 1917 was one of the few established writers who rallied at once to the Soviet regime. Wrote *Mystery Buffo*, 1918, a verse play prophesying victory of Revolution over capitalism, but his later satirical plays, *The Bedbug*, 1928, and *The Bath House*, 1929, show disillusionment with the growing philistinism and bureaucracy of Soviet life. He was a poet of action and had a great passion for truth, but the shafts of his satire were directed equally against friend and foe. In 1918–20 contributed drawings and texts for thousands of propaganda posters. In 1923 joined the Russian Association of Proletarian Writers (Rapp), the agency of Party control over literature, and made a tremendous effort to do what was officially wanted, fervently promising to write "a hundred Party books." Only two months later, however, he shot himself without having written another line except his death-note (in which he said: "The boat of love has crashed on the rocks of everyday life").

METNER, EMILE KARLOVICH (1872–1936). Philosopher and philologist. Emigrated and died in Dresden.

Moscow. Moscow is encircled by two "rings"—the Boulevard, near the center of town, and, beyond that, the Sadovaya. Before the Revolution the industrial and working-class areas were mainly in the outskirts, beyond the Sadovaya ring. The area inside this ring was mostly occupied by offices, shops, theaters, hotels, the University, etc. Two main working-class areas were the Presnya district to the west of the Sadovaya ring, and the "railway district" around the main-line termini, to the northwest (these were the chief storm centers during the 1905 Revolution). Tverskie and Yamskie Streets and Oruzheyny Lane are just beyond the Sadovaya ring to the northwest, and Razgulyay Square is to the east. The Arbat, running west from the Boulevard ring through the Sadovaya ring, and Myasnitsky Street, cutting through both rings in the opposite direction, are mentioned in 1898 and 1903 guides to Moscow as lively streets with elegant houses and foreign shops. "Truba" is what Muscovites called the area around Trubnaya Square, on the north sector of the Boulevard ring. There was a market there, for birds, fishermen's equipment, etc. The Tsvetnoi Boulevard, just north of the Truba, is divided into two lanes with gardens between them; the Circus and the Central Market were in this boulevard. Yushkov Lane was a turning off Myasnitsky Street just before it crossed the Boulevard ring. Okhotny Ryad was the game market, near the very center of Moscow. The Church of Sts. Florus and

Laurus was on Myasnitsky Street. The saints are recognized only by the Greek Orthodox Church. They are said to have been stonemasons who were martyred in Illyria in the second century because they erected a cross on a heathen temple that they had been ordered to build. Their saints' day is August 18th.

MURATOV, PAVEL PAVLOVICH (1881–1950). Novelist and critic. Associated with the periodical *The World of Art,* which was founded in 1898 by Diaghilev and became the center of the aesthetic movement in art and literature. Author of a *History of Old Russian Painting,* 1914. Emigrated.

MUSAGET (i.e., Musagetes, Apollo, leader of the Muses). Publishing house, founded in 1909, which published a symbolist review of the same name.

MYASOYEDOV, GRIGORY GRIGORIEVICH (1835–1911). Painter. Studied abroad. On return he became one of the organizers of the Society for Travelling Art Exhibitions. His paintings deal with peasant life and historical episodes. Member of the Academy of Art from 1893.

NADIRADZE, KOLAU (NIKOLAY) (1894–   ). Georgian poet. Born at Kutais, studied at Moscow University. First verses appeared in 1916 in the journal of the Georgian symbolists, *Blue Horns.* There is a great deal of mysticism and nationalistic romanticism in his writings. After Sovietization of Georgia, Nadiradze was at first hostile, but later wrote on revolutionary themes.

NATALYA NIKOLAYEVNA (PUSHKIN), NÉE GONCHAROV. Alexander Pushkin's wife. Pushkin met her in Moscow when she was only seventeen and married her a year later, on February 18, 1831. There were two sons and two daughters of the marriage. Pushkin was killed six years later, on January 29, 1837, in a duel with a cavalry officer, Dantès, an adopted son of the Dutch ambassador, whom he suspected of having an affair with his wife.

NEP. The New Economic Policy of the Soviet government, promulgated in May, 1921, by which the rigid state control of industry and agriculture was relaxed.

NILENDER, V. O. Poet and translator. Member of Society of Religious Philosophy.

Niva. Weekly illustrated magazine for family reading, published in Petersburg from 1870 to 1918 by A. F. Marx. Attained a circulation exceeding 200,000. Published supplements, including works of Turgenev, Goncharov, and Dostoevsky. Published works by L. N. Tolstoy, including *Resurrection,* which was serialized in 1899, Nos. 11–52.

OSTROVSKY, ALEXANDER NIKOLAYEVICH (1823–86). Famous Russian dramatist closely associated with the Maly Theater in Moscow.

PASTERNAK, BORIS LEONIDOVICH (1890–   ). Poet and novelist. Born in Moscow, eldest son of Leonid Pasternak, the painter, and Rosa Pasternak, née Kaufman, the pianist. In 1901 enters secondary school in Moscow. Meets Scriabin in summer of 1903 and decides to take up music as a career. First visit abroad, to Germany, with family in 1906. Enters Moscow University (Faculty of Law) in 1908. Scriabin returns to Russia in 1909 and Pasternak changes over from Law to Philosophy on his advice. Becomes member of Serdarda circle and the Musaget group of writers, poets, and critics in 1910. Spends summer term at Marburg University, studying Kantian philosophy under Hermann Cohen, 1912. After abortive love affair, which he describes in *Safe Conduct,* decides to give up philosophy and devote himself to poetry. Graduates from Moscow University in spring, 1913, and in summer of the same year writes most of his first book of poems, *A Twin in the Clouds,* published in the autumn of 1914. Joins the Centrifugue futurists' association in spring and meets Mayakovsky in May, 1914. Tutor to son of Moscow manufacturer, 1914 to 1916. Meets Khlebnikov, founder of Russian futurism in October, 1915. Spends two winters (1915–1917) doing clerical work in ordnance factories in the Urals and returns to Moscow in March, 1917. Publishes second book of verse, *Above the Barriers,* and writes and loses ms. of the *Reverse of the Medal.* Writes third book of verse, *My Sister, Life,* in summer, 1917. Writes two short stories, *The Childhood of Luverse* and *Letters from Tula,* in 1918. Breaks with Mayakovsky in 1920, meets Alexander Blok in Moscow in 1921. Pasternak's parents and sisters leave for Berlin in 1921, and Pasternak works as salesman in Writers' Bookshop in Moscow. *My Sister, Life,* published in 1921. First marriage, 1922; leaves with wife for Berlin to visit parents and prepare publication of fourth book of verse; revisits Marburg. Publishes fourth collection of verse, *Themes and Variations,* in Berlin and Moscow and returns to Moscow in autumn. In 1924, works in library of People's Commissariat of Foreign Affairs; 1925, publishes four short stories in book form, *Childhood of Luverse, Letters from Tula, Il Tratto di Apelle,* and *Aerial Ways.* In 1927, publishes in book form two revolutionary poems: *The Year 1905* and *Lieutenant Schmidt,* as well as *A Story.* In 1929–31, publishes first autobiography, *Safe Conduct,* in serial form. Mayakovksy commits suicide, February 14, 1930. Friendship with Paolo Yashvili, 1930–31. Divorce and remarriage, early 1930's. Stays in Georgia and works on translations of Georgian poets. Publishes *Spektorsky,* a novel in verse, in 1931, as well as a collection of verse for children, *The Zoo.* In 1932, publishes a volume of collected poems, *Second Birth.* During the years from 1932 to 1943 works mainly as translator. In June, 1935, attends first anti-Fascist congress in Paris and meets Marina Tsvetayeva and her family. In 1937, death of Paolo Yashvili and of Titian Tabidze. Publishes translation of *Hamlet,* 1940. Suicide of Marina Tsvetayeva, 1941. During Second World War (1941–45) publishes patriotic war poems and continues work on translations of Shakespeare. In 1943, publication of collected poems, *In Early Trains,* and 1945 publication of collected poems, *Wide Open Spaces of the Earth.* In 1946, Zhdanov's attack on cosmopolitanism in literature imposes renewed silence on Pasternak as poet. In 1950, publication of translation of Goethe's *Faust.* Publishes ten poems from *Doctor Zhivago* in *Znamya.* Submits manuscript of *Doctor Zhivago* to the editorial board of *Novy Mir* in summer, 1956; novel rejected by *Novy Mir* editors in September, 1956. *Doctor Zhivago* first published abroad in Italian in autumn, 1957, and a year later in English in the United States and England.

Expelled from the Union of Soviet Writers in November, 1958, after award of Nobel Prize for Literature.

PASTERNAK, LEONID OSIPOVICH (1862–1945). Father of Boris Pasternak. Well-known painter and illustrator. After leaving Russia in 1921 lived first in Germany (Berlin and Munich) and from 1938 in England. Died in Oxford.

PASTERNAK, ROSA ISODORNOVNA, née Kaufman (1867–1940). Mother of Boris Pasternak. Well-known concert pianist. Gave up professional career when she married.

PETROVSKY, MIKHAIL ALEXEYEVICH (1887–   ). Critic and translator.

PILNYAK, pseudonym of Vogau, Boris Andreyevich (1894–1937). Novelist. First works published in 1915. His novel *The Naked Year,* 1922, deals with the Civil War, shows life degenerating to an animal level. His *Tale of the Unextinguished Moon,* 1926, gives an account of the death of Frunze, War Commissar, on the operating table in 1925, hinting that it was a "medical murder" ordered by Stalin. This got him into trouble from which he never recovered. His novel *Mahogany* was refused publication in Russia and he had it published in Berlin in 1929. This led to his expulsion from the Union of Soviet Writers. In 1937 he disappeared, and it is believed that he has been shot.

POLENOV, VASILY DMITRIEVICH (1844–1927). Painter. Paintings of country life. Took part as volunteer in Serbo-Turkish war of 1876 and as war artist in Russo-Turkish war of 1877–78. A member of the Society for Travelling Art Exhibitions. In the 1880's he painted a series of scenes from the life of Christ. Was elected a member of the Academy of Art in 1893. After the October Revolution lived in the country in a village now called Polenovo. Made People's Artist in 1926.

PRZYBYSZEWSKI, STANISLAW (1868–1927). Outstanding Polish romantic poet, of the 1890's and 1900's. After spending several years in Scandinavia and Germany he returned to Poland in 1898 and became editor of *Zycie,* the leading weekly of the modern poets. He wrote plays full of fatalistic terror and prose poems dealing with the mystical and tragic side of love and death, and these became the fashion of the day.

REBIKOV, VLADIMIR IVANOVICH (1866–1920). Composer. One of the first representatives of modernism in Russian music. Composed *Fables,* based on Krylov, and the opera *Christmas Tree,* based on Dostoevsky, as well as a number of lyrical pieces for the piano; performed as pianist both in Russia and abroad.

REPIN, ILYA YEFIMOVICH (1844–1930). Famous Russian painter. Studied in Petersburg, Italy, and Paris. Active in the Society for Travelling Art Exhibitions. His paintings deal with peasant life and many historical subjects, as *Ivan the Terrible with His Son Ivan,* 1885; *The Zaporozhian Cossacks Write to the Sultan,* 1891. His portraits include several of well-known Russian writers, composers, painters, and, among foreign celebrities, one of Eleonora Duse.

SADOVSKY, BORIS ALEXANDROVICH (1881–   ). Symbolist poet and critic.

SAPUNOV, NIKOLAY NIKOLAYEVICH (1880–1912). Painter. Studied under Levitan, Korovin, and Serov. Visited

Italy in 1902. Joined the Blue Rose group. Painted landscapes in Levitan's manner. Designed scenery for productions of Ibsen's *Hedda Gabler,* Blok's *Balalaika
Player,* Gozzi's *Turandot,* etc.

SCRIABIN, ALEXANDER NIKOLAYEVICH (1872–1915). Composer. Born in Moscow, son of diplomat and pianist.
Attended the aristocratic Cadet School. In 1882–92 at
the Moscow Conservatory studied composition with
Taneyev and piano with Safonov, winning a gold
medal as a pianist in 1892. In 1898–1903 professor of
the piano at Moscow Conservatory. His earlier compositions show a kinship with Chopin. His *Poème Sata-
nique* of 1903 echoes Liszt's *Malediction* and shows
Scriabin committing himself to the view of art as
magic. His First Symphony in 1901 already shows a
taste for the grandiose and the religious. With the
fourth of the piano sonatas, written in 1903, he has
thrown off the drawing-room elegance of his earlier
compositions and reveals the fragmentation of melody
and ecstatic trills of his maturer period. His idea of a
musical performance as a magic rite, a liturgical incanta-
tion and the calling to life of hidden cosmic forces, is
explicit in the inscription over the orgiastic Fifth Piano
Sonata: "I call you forth to life, hidden influences, sunk
in the obscure depths of the Creative Spirit, timid
germs of life, I bring you boldness!" He soon developed
an interest in theosophy and saw himself as the messiah
destined to bring about the Final Act, "the act of Union
between the Male-Creator and the Woman World," by
which Spirit was to redeem Matter, a great liturgical
rite in which all the arts were to play a part and which

was to usher in a new era. The nearest he approached to his idea was "the poem of fire," *Prometheus,* for orchestra, piano, and *clavier à lumières*—the first attempt to achieve a synthesis of the arts and a "counterpoint of the senses." He dreamed of "a musical phrase ending in a scent, a chord that resolved itself into a color, a melodic line whose climax becomes a caress." He saw himself as Prometheus, the Free Redeemer, rescuing the world of Matter by the power of Spirituality, hence his *Poem of Ecstasy (Poème de l'extase),* his most famous composition. Between 1904 and 1910 he toured Switzerland, France (where he first became acquainted with the writings of Blavatsky and Annie Besant), Italy, and the United States. In 1910 he performed in Holland and in 1914 in Britain. Died prematurely of an infection of the blood. In 1922 his apartment in Moscow was made a museum of his life and work.

SELVINSKY, ILYA LVOVICH (1899–   ). Poet. Leader of the "constructivist" group which sought to subordinate the imagery and vocabulary of poetry to its theme. In 1929–30 the constructivist movement rallied a number of poets to a program of active support for the regime. At one time it seemed that Selvinsky might take Mayakovsky's place. His first poems appeared in 1926. Of his later work, his ballads and songs have been the most successful. In 1933–34 he took part in the Arctic expedition of the *Chelyuskin* and wrote a poem about this. During the 1941–45 war, wrote patriotic verses.

SERAPION FRATERNITY. The Serapion group came together in 1921, taking their name from the hermit Serapion in Hoffmann's stories, in whose cave a variety of people gather and tell each other their experiences. The group included Tikhonov, Fedin, and Vsevolod Ivanov. It played an important part in restoring normal literary activity after a period of chaos and disorder and in bringing together older and experienced writers with young writers who, demobilized from the Civil War, were determined to pursue a literary career.

SEROV, VALENTIN ALEXANDROVICH (1865-1911). Painter. Born in Petersburg, son of the composers A. N. Serov and V. S. Serova. Pupil of Repin. Especially distinguished as portrait painter, but also painted scenes of country life and dramatic compositions, such as *The Meeting: An Exile's Wife Arrives*. At the end of the nineteenth century, Serov joined the World of Art group. During the 1905 Revolution drew caricatures for the revolutionary press, sent protest to the Academy of Art against the massacre of January 9th, and resigned from the Academy when it was rejected. Portraits of actresses Yermolova and Feodotova, also of Chaliapin and Stanislavsky.

SEVERYANIN, IGOR, pseudonym of Lotaryov, Igor Vasilyevich (1887-1941). Poet. Leader of the symbolist group called "Ego-Futurists." Emigrated after the Revolution. Was in Estonia when it was occupied by the Soviet Union in 1940, and wrote verses hailing the Soviet power. His poetry idealizes the aspirations of the average townsman. His claim to be a futurist was based on his love of such things as cars and luxury hotels, and on his profuse coining of new words—most of which were in complete disharmony with the genius of the language.

SHCHEGOLEV, PAVEL YELISEYEVICH (1877-1931). Historian of Russian literature.

SHENROK, VLADIMIR IVANOVICH (1853–1910). Historian of literature. Specialized in the study of Gogol.

SHERSHENEVICH, VADIM GAVRILOVICH (1893–1942). Poet. First works were close to the symbolists. Later wrote about urban life in the futurist manner. In 1919–24 joined the imagists, wrote verses which are catalogues of metaphors, not linked by any unity of poetic idea. Translator of Shakespeare, Corneille, and Baudelaire. Author of film scenarios, libretti for operettas, etc.

SIMONOV, KONSTANTIN MIKHAILOVICH (1915–   ). Soviet poet, novelist, and playwright. His earlier verse was mostly love poetry. Graduated from the literary institute of the Union of Soviet Writers in 1938. Wrote a patriotic poem about Suvorov, 1939. During the Second World War became the most popular lyric poet. Wrote novels about the war: *Days and Nights, Comrades in Arms,* as well as plays, including the anti-American play, *The Russian Question.* Since the war mainly active in journalism as editor of *Literaturnaya Gazeta* and *Novy Mir.* Is now under a cloud, following the disgrace of Fadeyev.

SOCIETY FOR TRAVELLING ART EXHIBITIONS (*Peredvizhniki*). On November 9, 1863, thirteen pupils of the Academy of Art who were all Gold Medallist candidates refused to paint a picture on the set subject of *Odin in Valhalla.* They grouped themselves into an Artists' Co-operative Society, and in 1870, thanks to the financial assistance of Tretyakov, a rich patron of the arts, founded the Society for Travelling Art Exhibitions. The society undertook to educate the masses by means of their exhibitions, which they held in the capitals, in Kiev, Odessa, Riga, Kazan, etc. The critical writings of

V. V. Stasov were sympathetic to this activity and indeed furnished its ideology. Members of the society included the brothers Vasnetsov, Levitan, V. E. Makovsky, Polenov, Repin, Serov, Surikov.

SOLOVYOV, VLADIMIR SERGEYEVICH (1853–1900). Poet, critic, and most influential of nineteenth-century Russian religious philosophers. Was the son of a distinguished historian. He had apocalyptic dreams of the end of the world, and appears to have believed literally in the coming of Antichrist. His poetry gave expression to the symbolist belief that the world is a system of symbols which express the existence of the abstract metaphysical realities. While working at the Reading Room of the British Museum he had a vision of Sophia, Divine Wisdom. He had another such vision later in Egypt. His idea of the World Soul is satirized by Chekhov in *The Seagull.*

SOMOV, KONSTANTIN NIKOLAYEVICH (1869–1939). Painter and art critic. Member of the World of Art group.

STASOV, VLADIMIR VASILYEVICH (1824–1906). Art and music critic. Keen supporter of the Society for Travelling Art Exhibitions. In the 1880's wrote a number of works on the history of art. Edited the published letters of Musorgsky and Glinka.

STEPUN, F. A. (1885–   ). Producer. One of the founders in 1919 of the State Exemplary Theater in Moscow, with the aim of educating the masses through the great classics, including Shakespeare and the tragedies of antiquity. Author of an adaptation of Sophocles' *Oedipus Rex* intended to demonstrate that ancient Thebes showed the tragedy of contemporary Russia. Attacked

by Meyerhold for his reactionary ideology, Stepun left
the Exemplary Theater. He now lives in Germany.
Author of *The Russian Soul and Revolution* and articles on stagecraft.

SUDEIKIN, SERGEY YURIEVICH (1883–   ). Artist, participant
in the exhibitions of the Blue Rose and the World of
Art groups. His pictures, mainly landscapes, are mostly
studies for theatrical scenery. Exhibited in Paris, 1921.

SUPREME COUNCIL OF NATIONAL ECONOMY (V.S.N.). Set up
in 1917 as supreme economic organ of the dictatorship
of the proletariat. Reorganized in 1932 into separate
People's Commissariats of Heavy Industry, Light Industry, and Timber Industry.

SURIKOV, VASILY IVANOVICH (1848–1916). Painter. A member
of the Society for Travelling Art Exhibitions. Studied
in Petersburg but quarrelled with his conservative professors and moved to Moscow in 1877. Great historical
pictures are *The Morning of the Execution of the
Streltsi*, 1881, *Menshikov at Beryozov*, 1883, *The Boya-
rina Morozova*, 1887. Scenes from the careers of Stenka
Razin and Pugachov.

TABIDZE, TITIAN JUSTINOVICH (1895–1937). Poet. One of the
founders of the Georgian symbolist group Blue Horns,
1915. Rallied to the Soviet power after 1921, and wrote
poetry glorifying the struggle to transform the Colchis
marshes into citrus fruit plantations. The Blue Horns
group was criticized at Congress of Soviet Writers in
1934 as "fellow-travellers." Tabidze was shot in one of
the purges of the thirties.

THIRD ROME. After the Grand Dukes of Russia had assumed the title of Tsar, Moscow (then the capital) was called the "Third Rome," the "First" being Rome itself and the "Second," Byzantium.

TIKHONOV, A. N. Editor. Published some of Pasternak's poetry and prose in his journal *Russky Sovremennik* in the 1920's.

TIKHONOV, NIKOLAI SEMYONOVICH (1896–). Prominent Soviet poet. Fought in the First World War and the Civil War (on the Red side). His first poems were war poems written in 1916 and 1917. His next two books of poems, *The Horde* and *Country Beer,* came out in 1922. Characteristic feature of his later poetry is its universality. His volume of poems *The Shadow of a Friend* includes poems written in Poland, Austria, France, Belgium, and England, while in his two volumes of verse *Yurga* and *Poems of Kakhetia* are contained his experiences in the Caucasus and Soviet Central Asia. He is greatly attracted by strong personalities, grandiose scenery, and enterprises involving risk and danger. His experiences in beleaguered Leningrad are described in the volume of his war poems, *The Fiery Year.*

TOLSTOY, ALEXEY KONSTANTINOVICH (1817–1875). Poet and dramatist. Moscow Art Theater opened its first season with his play *Tsar Fyodor Ioanovich* in October, 1898.

TOLSTOY, ANDREY LVOVICH (1877–1916). Leo Tolstoy's ninth child.

TOLSTOY, ILYA LVOVICH (1866–1933). Leo Tolstoy's third child, second son. Author of *Reminiscences of My Father.*

TOLSTOY, SERGEY LVOVICH (1863–1947). Leo Tolstoy's eldest son. Author of monograph on father, *My Father in the Seventies.*

TRETYAKOV, SERGEY MIKHAILOVICH (1892–1939). Soviet dramatist, author of *Roar, China!*, produced by Meyerhold. Arrested during the purges of 1937–38 and disappeared.

TRUBETSKOY, PAVEL PETROVICH (1867–1938). Born and died in Italy. Famous Russian sculptor. Lived in Russia 1897–1906, also paid some visits to Russia in 1907–14. Worked in France and U.S.A. Statuettes: *L. N. Tolstoy on Horseback*, 1899; *A Moscow Cabby*, 1898; *Girl with a Dog*, 1901. The equestrian monument to Alexander III in Petersburg, unveiled in 1909.

TSVETAYEVA, MARINA IVANOVNA (1892–1941). Poet. Began her literary work in 1910. Left Russia in 1922, to be with her husband, a former White officer, first in Czechoslovakia, later in Paris. Returned with family to Russia in 1939. Her husband was arrested and punished. Their daughter, too, was arrested, and their son was killed early in the war. Tsvetayeva was banished to the provinces, where she could find no employment, and hanged herself. Her poems are distinguished by their exhilarating rhythm, fire, and passion, and by their strong folk-song influences.

TVARDOVSKY, ALEXANDER TRIFONOVICH (1910–   ). Soviet poet. First publication of his poems was in 1930. He achieved fame with his three long narrative poems, *The Land of Muravia, Vasily Tyorkin,* and *The House by the Roadside.* His realism is highly imaginative, the realism of pure poetry where everything is possible, where, for instance, the agony of war, which is the main theme of *Vasily Tyorkin,* finds expression in the dialogue between the Soldier and Death, and in *The House by the Roadside* where the rights of the human personality are voiced by the new-born baby in its dialogue with its mother.

TYUTCHEV, FYODOR IVANOVICH (1803–73). Russian lyric poet. He wrote about three hundred short lyric poems. His poetry is rich in imagery of vision and sound.

ULYANOV, NIKOLAY PAVLOVICH (1875–1949). Painter. Studied in Moscow under Serov, who influenced him a great deal. His portraits include one of Chekhov and one of Stanislavsky. He did a great deal of work for the theater, designing the sets for *Les Fourberies de Scapin, The Days of the Turbins, Carmen*. His memoirs were published posthumously in 1952.

VANNOVSKY, PYOTR SEMYONOVICH (1822–1904). Minister of Education who, in his modernization program, added to the science curriculum.

VASNETSOV, APPOLLINARY MIKHAILOVICH (1856–1933). Painter. Born in Vyatka province, son of a village priest. Joined the Society for Travelling Art Exhibitions and became well known as a landscape painter, especially of Ural and Siberian scenes. From 1890 lived in Moscow and painted pictures illustrating the city's historic past. Elected to Academy in 1900. Designed scenery for operas *Khovanshchina, Sadko,* etc. Published a book on art, 1908, in which he attacked impressionism. After the October Revolution became chairman of the Commission for the Study of Old Moscow and devoted himself mainly to archaeological work.

VASNETSOV, VIKTOR MIKHAILOVICH (1848–1926). Painter. Born in Vyatka province, son of a village priest. Elder

brother of Appollinary. Associated with Repin and
V. V. Stasov. Painted scenes of the life of the city poor
in a realistic vein. In 1878 moved to Moscow. Painted
subjects from Russian folklore and medieval history,
notably a portrait of *Ivan the Terrible,* and the group
Bogatyri, reproduced often. In the 1880's did scenery
and costumes for the theater and opera. Elected to the
Academy in 1893.

VERHAËREN, EMILE (1855–1916). Belgian poet. Began publishing verse in Brussels in the 1880's. Much influenced
by the impressionist painters. Some of his verses described the Belgian countryside and lamented the flight
of population to the towns and the expansion of the
great industrial towns into the countryside. His chief
work, *Toute la Flandre,* is a series of poems in which
autobiography is mingled with Flemish history and de-
scriptions of the Flemish scene. He also wrote love
poems, and some plays on historical and classical themes.

VRUBEL, MIKHAIL ALEXANDROVICH (1856–1910). Painter.
Member of the Academy of Art from 1905. Well known
as book illustrator and theatrical designer.

WORLD OF ART, THE. A group of painters and writers including all the symbolists supporting the review of the
same name (1899–1904). Had no common program but
were all united against the tendencies prevalent in the
Russian Academy of Art and the Society for Travelling
Art Exhibitions.

YAKUNCHIKOVA, MARIA VASILYEVNA (1870–1902). Artist,
studied in Moscow and Paris. Turned to decorative
art, and did many drawings for book covers, designs

for toys, etc. Painted a number of landscape pictures in a style similar to Levitan's.

YASHVILI, PAOLO DZHIBRAELOVICH (1895–1937). Georgian poet. Studied at Kutais *gymnasium,* wrote verses while still a schoolboy. On eve of First World War went to Paris. Returning home in 1916, Yashvili was one of the initiators of a group of Georgian symbolist poets. His poems—*Letter to Mother, The Red Bull*—were outstanding representative works of this group. Yashvili welcomed the establishment of Soviet power, and wrote poetry celebrating it. His verses on the death of Lenin were especially appreciated. In the 1930's he wrote about triumphs of socialist construction in Georgia, new hydroelectric plants, etc. Translated Pushkin, Lermontov, and Mayakovsky into Georgian. Committed suicide.

YEFREM OF SYRIA, ST. (Ephraem Syrus). A fourth-century Churchman who was born in Mesopotamia. Widely famous as a poet and a defender of orthodoxy against heretics. His writings were translated into Greek, Armenian, Coptic, Arabic, and Ethiopic. Most of his works were written in meter, and they include a number of hymns; he was distinguished among contemporary theological writers for the richness of his diction and his skill in the use of metaphors and illustrations.

ZABOLOTSKY, NIKOLAY (1903–   ). Poet. His early poems sounded like parodies or nonsense verse, but after a disappearance of several years he returned and wrote in a more orthodox style.